Praise for Moore

'A window into the past when barefoot kids could be seen among the second-hand clothes and furniture stalls, the rabbit sellers, butchers and vegetable traders – a wonderful book, not just for the pictures from a century ago but for the history of the entire area.'

Irish Independent

'This lavishly illustrated work documents the street's history, personalities and stories and is a fitting tribute to a great part of our capital.'

Irish Mail on Sunday

'One of the most colourful places in our capital city and now the sights and sounds of Moore Street have been captured in this book.'

Irish Mirror

'A book that captures the rich history of one of Dublin's most famous streets.'

Dublin People

'This is a wonderful book filled with the sights and sounds of the city and a collection of very evocative photos.'

Irish Catholic

Moore Street *c*.1960.
(Courtesy of the Irish Independent*)*

MOORE STREET

The Story of Dublin's Market District

BARRY KENNERK

MERCIER PRESS

IRISH PUBLISHER – IRISH STORY

MERCIER PRESS

Cork

www.mercierpress.ie

ISBN: 978 1 78117 177 6

10 9 8 7 6 5 4 3 2 1

A CIP record for this title is available from the British Library

The author and publisher gratefully acknowledge permission granted to reproduce copyrighted photographs used in this book. Every effort has been made to trace the copyright holders and to obtain their permission for the use of such material. The author and publisher apologise for any errors or omissions and would be grateful to receive notification of corrections for incorporation into future reprints or editions.

Printed and bound in Spain by GraphyCems.

In memory of Seamus Scully

Contents

Moore Street, July 2012.
(Author's collection)

Foreword

Moore Street: Mischievous Mascot of the Nation

Joe Duffy

If I was to pick one place to represent our country – somewhere that captures its history, people, sounds, smells and colours – it would have to be Moore Street. Located at the heart of our national psyche, it nestles in the shadow of O'Connell Street like a good-humoured, lucky, but mischievous mascot. From Molly Malone to the cheeky Charlie, not to mention the gurrier, the quare fella or the bowsie, Moore Street embraces all these wonderful characteristics and more. The ever-shifting kaleidoscope of the market mirrors our changing demography – if you want to know what Ireland looks like on any given day, slip down to Moore Street.

My earliest memory of the market stems from around 1966. We had just completed our annual Christmas trip to Woolworth's in Henry Street, where I had my first 'restaurant meal' of gravy, sausages, mash and onions, followed by one of their unique creamy cornets downstairs and a bag of iced gems. Afterwards, we headed around to Moore Street to get a schoolbag – I can recall savouring the sweet deep smell of the new leather.

Not only did the street teem with vegetable, fish and meat stalls, elbowing each other for precious space, but it was also tightly packed with fantastic shops that seemed to teeter on top of each other.

It was here, aged ten, that I first met broadcaster Gabriel Mary Byrne as he left the RTÉ radio studios in the GPO. As he walked back to his Triumph Herald sports car, clutching a brown leather zip-up briefcase under his arm, I ran up in my short trousers and little Duke shoes to ask for his autograph. He duly scribbled it for a relatively small fee!

Later, I got my first job as a lift boy in the Metropole cinema, restaurant and ballroom complex. As a curious thirteen-year-old, I used to spend my lunch hours rambling around Moore Street. To me, all human life was there. The 'dealers' were seen as a hardy bunch of women – 'if you don't want them, don't maul them son'. Here was a world where men worked for women, hauling fruit and veg by horse and cart to the makeshift stalls which the females controlled with the sharp side of an orange box and an iron fist.

When I found myself elected president of Trinity College Students' Union in 1979 with a bedsit in the college, guess where the nearest and cheapest groceries could be found? My beloved Moore Street of course. F. X. Buckley's, Hanlon's and Sheils' all provided good, affordable meat, while the stalls on the street yielded up fruit and vegetables.

In 1984 eleven Dunne's Stores workers in Henry Street were sacked for refusing to handle produce from apartheid South Africa. As president of the Union of Students in Ireland, I joined them on the picket line as they fought for their jobs. Afterwards, myself and the deputy president, Northerner Mark Durkan, used to head around to Moore Street for our weekly shop (vegetables and smoked cod) before walking back to the house we shared in Great Western Square.

I know the street is not the same; everything changes. Gay Byrne's autograph prices are now beyond everyone's reach, but Moore Street still retains the flavour of the nation, reflecting the people of the country better than any census ever could. Long may Moore Street flow through our veins, no matter where we find ourselves.

Barry Kennerk loves Dublin and, above all, its people; he has a great record of championing unsung heroes and heroines, reminding us that our streets are steeped in real history. Flesh-and-blood memories are embedded in this wonderful book – savour this fantastic addition to our nation's history.

Preface

The traders of Moore Street have long held a place in Dublin's cultural heart, but what is sometimes forgotten is that their market is a constantly changing place. Today the stalls that remain are just a small remnant of a much larger market that once existed there. What started in the mid eighteenth century as a residential district gave way to a bazaar of back streets and alleys, each specialising in a particular type of trade: second-hand clothing, furniture, small game, fruit, vegetables, poultry and larger meats. It provided an important lifeline for generations of Dubliners, as well as for the country people who flocked there each Christmas. In their turn, the traders had their own lifeline in the North Circular Road cattle market, as well as in the covered markets at nearby Halston Street – one dealing in fish and the other in flowers, fruit and vegetables.

Over a century ago, my great-grandfather, Con Kennerk, lived in the heart of the market. His own mother, Eliza Brady, came from Cole's Lane, where her father was a furniture broker. In 1908 Con returned to the market with his family from Usher's Quay, first taking up residence at a house in Norfolk Market and then at Little Denmark Street. During the day, his wife, Maggie Austin, ran a shop at No. 23, where she sold everything from sweets to coal. The family had first-hand experience of the 1916 Rising and of the War of Independence that followed. In later years, my father and his siblings played around the slaughterhouses of the Lime Yard (Market Street).

As I attempted to uncover their story – one played out amid the stalls of Dublin's very own *souk* – I found that written accounts of Moore Street, occasionally excellent, were nevertheless disparate, and that its oral history was fragmentary: a consequence perhaps of the complete dissolution of the market community from the 1950s onwards.

In an effort to remedy this, I chose to divide this book into three distinct sections. The first takes a thematic look at some of the events that have helped to shape development in the market since the early eighteenth century. The second introduces seven 'voices of Moore Street', each representing a different aspect of life there. The last part of the book is a street-by-street account of the wider market area, its people and its buildings.

Overall it is dedicated to historian and member of the Old Dublin Society Seamus Scully, who lived on Moore Street during the early part of the twentieth century. It is a remarkable testament to his research that even today historians writing about this part of Dublin continue to refer to his work. Scully, who knew Seán O'Casey and Elizabeth O'Farrell, lived out his final years in a modest little flat in Ballybough. He opened his home to anyone who was interested in Irish history.

I hope that this book does justice to his memory, as well as to those traders who are still in business. They may well regard this book with a mix of interest and bemusement. After all, for the past 100 years they and their predecessors have been interviewed endlessly – their reactions serving as a local gauge for international events such as the Second World War, or Ireland's entry into the European Union. Immortalised in poems and songs, they watch the people come and go – one eye on the stall, a finger on the steady pulse of city life.

Acknowledgements

So many people helped to make this project possible. Since a large portion of the book relies on visual imagery, due recognition needs to be given to photographer Mr Tommy Nolan, who took the time to visit Moore Street with me. Thereafter, I reserve acknowledgement for the Irish Architectural Archive, the National Library of Ireland, the Royal Society of Antiquaries of Ireland and Dublin City Library and Archive. I would also like to thank Paul Ferguson of the Trinity College Map Library and the staff of the Irish Military Archives.

A special mention goes to Gregory O'Connor of the National Archives of Ireland, without whom I would not have known about the Property Losses (Ireland) Committee files of 1916, and to *Ireland's Own* and the *Evening Herald* for helping me to get in touch with Dubliners about their stories of Moore Street. Thereafter, a large number of individuals lent their support. In all, over thirty were interviewed. Not all can be mentioned here, but they are all quoted in the text. In addition, I would like to thank Shane Kenna, Colin White, Paddy Fetherston, Imelda and Margaret Buckley, Sally Anne Timmons of the Moore Street Lending Library project, retired butcher Eamon Martin, Terry Fagan, architect Cathal Crimmins and the members of the Save Moore Street campaign.

A number of people gave assistance with regard to the section on 1916. These include Fearghal McGarry, the webmaster of www.easterrising.eu and Shane MacThomáis, historian for the Glasnevin Trust.

Last, but not least, I wish to extend my warmest thanks to the editorial and design team at Mercier Press for their hard work. From start to finish this project has been a collaborative effort – something that is evident on every page of this book.

Craft **butchers**
Associated Craft Butchers of Ireland

I would like to thank specially the Associated Craft Butchers of Ireland, who very kindly provided financial support for the use of images in this book.

Moore Street, 1952.
(Courtesy of the Military Archives)

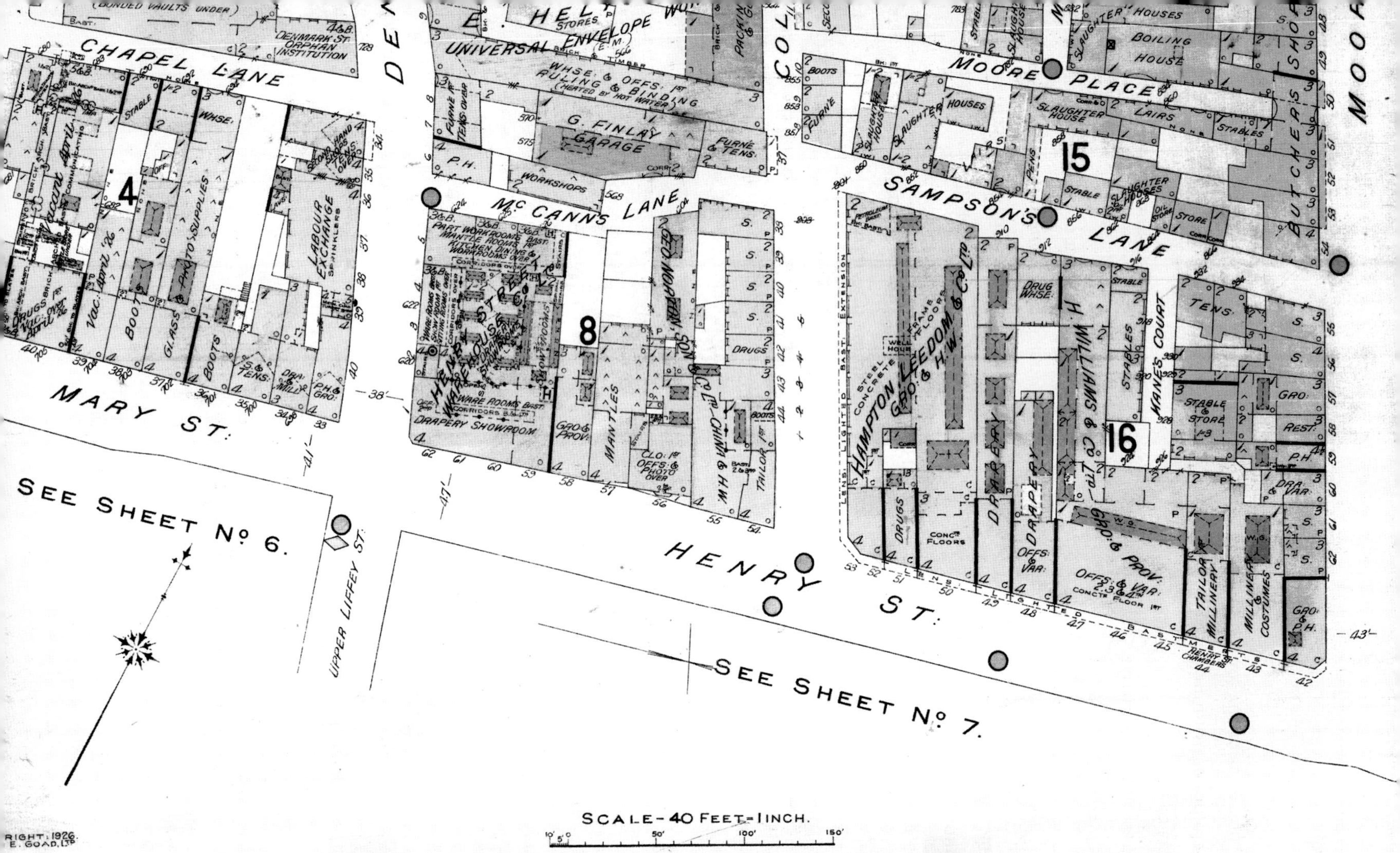

SEE SHEET No. 6.

SEE SHEET No. 7.

SCALE – 40 FEET – 1INCH.

MARY ST.

CHAPEL LANE

HENRY ST.

McCANN'S LANE

SAMPSON'S LANE

MOORE PLACE

UPPER LIFFEY ST.

DEN

DRUGS

PHOTO SUPPLIES

GLASS

BOOTS

BOOTS

LABOUR EXCHANGE
SPRINKLERS

Vac. April '26

4

UNIVERSAL ENVELOPE

GARAGE
G FINLAY

GEO. NORTON

CHINA & H.W.

TAILOR

MANTLES

DRAPERY SHOWROOM

8

HAMPTON LEEDOM & CO LTD

DRUGS

DRAPERY

DRAPERY

H WILLIAMS & CO LTD

STABLES

HANES COURT

TAILOR
MILLINERY

MILLINERY
COSTUMES

16

15

SLAUGHTER HOUSE

DOILING
HOUSE

BUTCHER'S SHO

MOOR

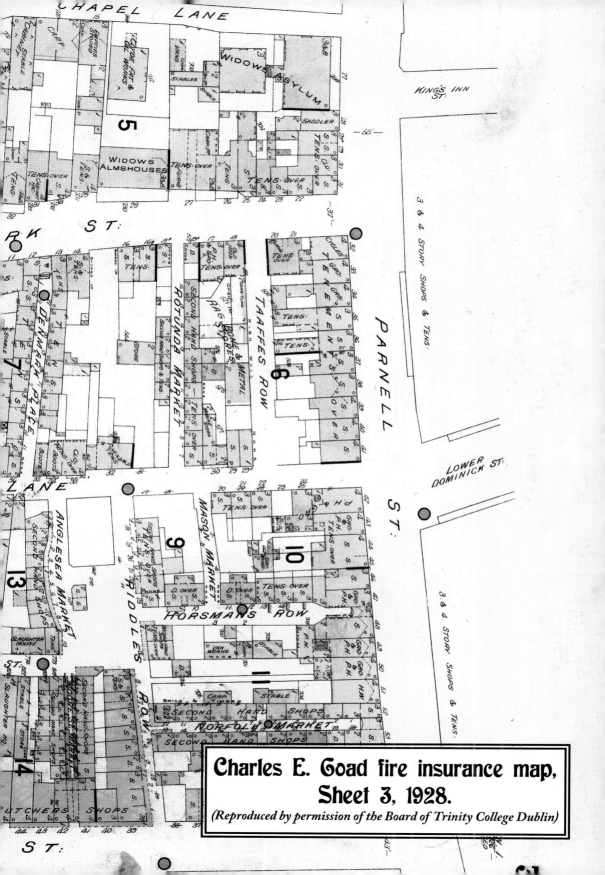

Charles E. Goad fire insurance map, Sheet 3, 1928.

(Reproduced by permission of the Board of Trinity College Dublin)

A dray loaded with cabbages leaves for Moore Street
c. 1940. *(Courtesy of Leonard & Sons)*

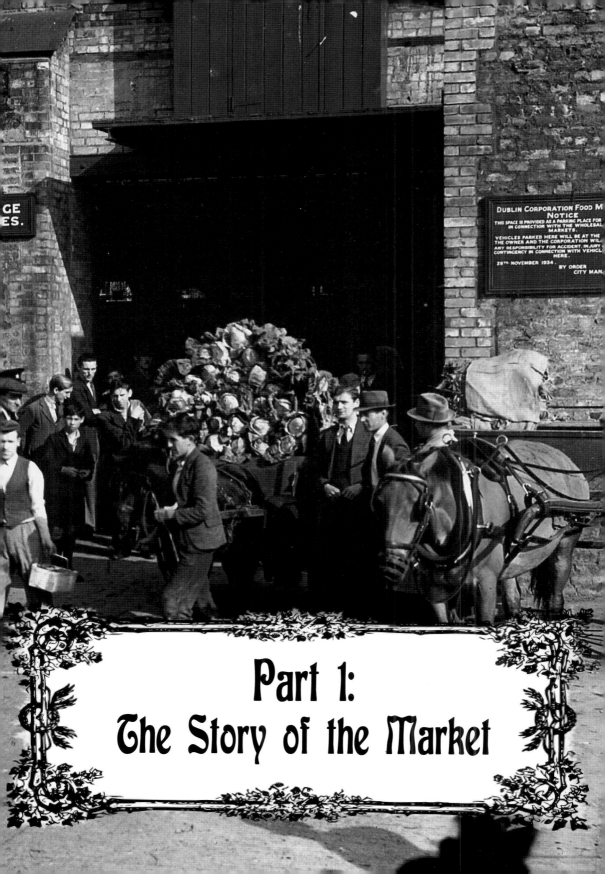

GE
ES.

DUBLIN CORPORATION FOOD M
NOTICE
THIS SPACE IS PROVIDED AS A PARKING PLACE FOR
IN CONNECTION WITH THE WHOLESAL
MARKETS.
VEHICLES PARKED HERE WILL BE AT THE
THE OWNER AND THE CORPORATION WIL
ANY RESPONSIBILITY FOR ACCIDENT, INJURY
CONTINGENCY IN CONNECTION WITH VEHICL
HERE.
28TH NOVEMBER 1934
BY ORDER
CITY MAN.

Part 1:
The Story of the Market

FINE Wall Cherries, ripe Wall Cherries.—A Penny a Quart, the ripe Gooseberries, a Penny a Quart.

Drawing from a 1775 Dublin broadsheet entitled 'The Dublin Cries or a representation of the various Cries and Callings throughout the Streets Lanes and Alleys of the City and Liberties of Dublin'. *(Courtesy of the National Library of Ireland)*

Luke Gardiner's Pantry

Markets have had a long history in the Moore Street area. Until the dissolution of the monasteries under King Henry VIII, much of the land along the north bank of the Liffey was owned by the monks of St Mary's Abbey, whose demesne extended into present-day Ballybough and Clonliffe. Such a large and influential site would naturally have attracted an open-air market, the existence of which is still recalled in the names of two local thoroughfares: Green Street and Little Green Street, just west of the Moore Street market area. Trade in the area was given further impetus by old city ordnances from the twelfth century that forbade the gutting of fish on the south bank of the river. Archaeological evidence suggests that as early as the Viking period fish were cured on open-air frames along the north bank, in a manner still seen in parts of Norway.

During the late seventeenth century, when the city's butchers and fishmongers were moved from south of the Liffey because of complaints about the stench, they returned to this area in large numbers. They were housed in the new purpose-built Ormond Market, constructed between 1682 and 1684 at the rear of Ormond Quay to a circular plan by Sir Humphrey Jervis. The market area adjoining Moore Street, which obtained its produce from Ormond Market, began to flourish during the mid to late eighteenth century. At that time several factors, such as the increasing cost of rent on Henry Street, caused grocers to migrate into the adjacent streets where overheads were cheaper. During the Georgian and Regency periods, the families of Dominick Street, Mountjoy Square and Rutland Square, with their large retinues of servants, provided a ready source of custom for the burgeoning market. The high cost of transporting fresh and easily spoilable produce such as meat and fruit to this open-air 'pantry' from further afield, meant that thrifty cooks needed to be able to buy their goods locally.

At that time, the city had a number of markets. These included Smithfield, where black cattle and sheep were sold, the wholesale fruit market at Little Green Street and Rotunda Market and Norfolk Market, which ran onto Great Britain (now Parnell) Street.

The widening of Drogheda Street to create Sackville (now O'Connell) Street by property developer Luke Gardiner in the mid 1750s gave additional impetus to the growth of the local meat and grocery trade. Before long, some of these traders began to advertise themselves as specialist dealers to the gentry. A lengthy poem called *The Joys of Saturday* describes a lady's shopping experience in the bustling market of Cole's Lane, giving some impression of how it must have been during the heyday of Georgian wealth:

> On through its throng fat dowagers are moving,
> Full well the butchers know each lady's name,
> And, while she gets along with careful shoving,
> Each doth the virtues of his beef proclaim;
>
> Her butcher now the knowing dame entreateth,
> Gravely he list'neth in his apron blue,
> And thus her coaxing and complaints he meeteth,
> 'I give it, ma'am, so cheap to none but you.'[1]

One verse describes how the poor room-keepers stood by until 'their betters are all served', with another introducing these worthies as 'butlers … and cooks of much importance'. For large transactions, a butcher's porter was on hand to take the meat home in a wicker basket. A species of pigeon known as the 'Easterling' was a popular buy, as were geese and turkeys.

Herrings appeared in the market from July to December. The Dublin Bay variety, with its distinctive green back, was particularly prized and could fetch a high price. Alongside these were salmon, caught at Islandbridge, and cod and ling, which came in from Newfoundland. They were frame-dried in fishing villages such as Rush and Skerries, before being packed in straw for transport.

Many types of fruit were also to be found in the market during Georgian times.

These included apples, pears and plums, as well as cherries when in season. Other fruits such as peaches, nectarines and pineapples were sold as the 'superfluity of gentlemen's gardens'.[2]

But all was not affluence. During the late eighteenth century, the city authorities had to contend with many of the same problems that would dog their Victorian descendants. During the 1780s, the area between Moore Street and Cole's Lane (later to include Norfolk, Mason's and Anglesea Markets) was known as Walsh's Market. It was less prosperous than the wider streets that bounded it. In 1781 a corporation supervisor reported that the inhabitants were 'raising the level of the street with rubbish, each striving to be higher than the other which has stopped the channel for the water, and is a nuisance'.[3] The road surface was levelled, and eight years later the city water-pipe supply was extended into the area – a set of works that also took in Smithfield and Sackville Street.[4]

Yet, despite these difficulties, the traders who worked along the narrow thoroughfares managed to produce meat and vegetable products of acceptable quality. They held something of a monopoly on the trade, the Rotunda Market off Little Denmark Street being the only one of its kind on the north-east side of the River Liffey. Already the seeds were being sown for generations of market trading.

Opposite: **Fruit-sellers by Samuel Frederick Brocas, c. 1820. *This page:* Women have always occupied a strong role in market life. Drawing of traders by Samuel Frederick Brocas, c. 1812. *(Courtesy of the National Library of Ireland)***

Regulation of the market area

For much of its history, the sheriff, working with the city corporation and lord mayor, had control over the market area. On 4 December 1725, *Faulkner's Dublin Journal* reported that, due to a scarcity of bread, 'His Lordship gives leave to all Persons whether Foreigners or Freemen to make and sell good Household Bread, in this City, and in the publick Market places upon all Days in the Week (Sundays excepted).'

In order to regulate trade in the market, the sheriff was required to summon a number of citizens at the general quarter sessions. Of these, three were empowered to examine goods on sale, reporting back to the lord mayor. He had the power to condemn putrid foodstuffs and to impose a £10 fine if necessary.

By the Victorian era, market trading was governed under the provisions of the Markets and Fairs Clauses Act 1847 (incorporated into the Dublin Improvement Act, 1849). The lord mayor continued to act as sole clerk. Under its auspices, Lord Mayor Benjamin Lee Guinness lost no time in making a number of by-laws. He was responsible for examining weights and measures, punishing fraudsters and collecting rents and stallage fees from corporation slaughterhouses throughout the city.

Fines were regularly administered. On 6 August 1873, Esther Harte, a Norfolk Market trader, was fined 5s 'for having incorrect measures for selling gooseberries'.[5] In July 1878 seven people had their scales confiscated.[6] Traders could also be penalised under the terms of the Iveagh Markets' Act for exposing clothes or furniture for sale on the footpath.[7] Trading was forbidden on the Sabbath, but occasionally some

ANNO VICESIMO QUARTO & VICESIMO QUINTO

VICTORIÆ REGINÆ.

****

Cap. ccxxxviii.

An Act for providing and constructing Markets, Market Places, and Slaughter-houses, with all necessary Conveniences, within the Parishes of *Saint Mary* and *Saint Bridget* in the City of Dublin.   [6th *August* 1861.]

WHEREAS the present Markets in the City of *Dublin* for the Sale of Meat, Fish, Butter, Bacon, Vegetables, and other Agricultural Produce, and of Eggs, Game, Fowls, and such like Articles, are insufficient for the Accommodation of the Inhabitants of the said City, and for the Purposes of those trading in the said Articles respectively: And whereas it is expedient to erect a new Market or Markets and Slaughter-houses, with other Offices and Buildings, One of such Markets to be situate on the North Side of the City of *Dublin* in the Parish of *Saint Mary*, on the Site of or near to the Market called " *Cole's Lane* Market," and the other of the said Markets on the South Side of the said City in the Parish of *Saint Bridget*, on the Site of or near to the Market called " the *Castle* Market," for the Sale of the said Articles: And whereas the said existing Markets and certain Lands and Houses adjacent thereto, as delineated on a Plan or Plans thereof which have been deposited as herein-after mentioned, would form suitable Sites

[*Local.*]   41 C   for

Extract from the Dublin General Markets Act (1861).

traders flouted this rule, as in the case of Thomas Mooney, a provision dealer from Riddall's Row who was charged in 1840 for 'keeping open for sale of goods on Sunday'.[8]

Other legislation governed the licensing, registration and inspection of slaughterhouses. The Dublin General Markets Act was passed in 1861, followed by a new set of by-laws in 1879. Each premises had to be properly ventilated, provided with an adequate supply of water and floored and skirted with asphalt over concrete to prevent the blood getting into the groundwater. Consideration was also given to the humane treatment of animals for slaughter. Section 7 stated: 'Every occupier of a slaughter-house shall cause every animal brought to such slaughter-house for the purpose of being slaughtered … to be provided … with a sufficient quantity of wholesome water and (if kept confined for more than twelve hours) food.' Each animal was to be 'felled with as little pain or suffering as practicable'. However, in the close confines of the Lime Yard (Market Street), Section 25 of the by-laws, which stated that slaughterhouses must be at least 100 feet away from dwellings, was hardly feasible.[9]

The area was also served by a local police force that worked alongside the

Anglesea Market, *c*. 1900. Traders were occasionally penalised under the terms of the Iveagh market act for exposing clothes and other items for sale on the footpath. *(Reproduced by permission of the Royal Society of Antiquaries of Ireland)*

corporation. During the eighteenth century, these were city watch officers, who carried pike staffs. They could be fined if their weapons were mislaid or stolen. A minute book for 1750–70 describes the way in which they worked the beat at the southern end of Sackville Mall: 'To patrol to Mrs Lassey's in Henry Street back to Off Lane [Henry Place], from thence to Doctor Robinson's round the Mall to his Stand.'[10]

When the Dublin Metropolitan Police was constituted as the city's constabulary in 1837, the old watch premises at 8 Henry Street became the headquarters of C Division. Officers were responsible for investigating all sorts of misdemeanours, including the keeping of shebeens, recovery of stolen property and the removal of unlicensed traders. In October 1840 the blind street balladeer Zozimus was arrested after he gathered 'a large crowd of persons in Cole's-lane market' to sing songs about the repeal of the Union. His appeal to the police magistrate at the court in Henry Street was a colourful one:

> Yer worship, I love my country, she's dear to my heart. And am I to be prevented from writing songs in her honour, as Tommy Moore, Walter Scott, aye, or Homer, have done for theirs, and of singing them after the manner of the ancient bard, save that I haven't a harp to accompany my aspirations?[11]

At other times crimes had a more political character, particularly when violent nationalism was at its height. During the 1860s several arms raids resulted in the recovery of revolvers and bowie knives.[12] Other crimes were perpetrated against livestock. *The Freeman's Journal* of 17 June 1870 records an early-morning incident at a slaughterhouse yard in Sampson's Lane in which five cows, a sheep and three lambs were killed with an axe.

Outside the immediate market confines, casual traders presented a problem for the city authorities. They had a roving licence that allowed them to sell throughout the borough of Dublin and they went where the custom was – theatre queues, hospital entrances or other places that might attract a healthy passing trade. It was very difficult to regulate them through the usual market by-laws, and they could be found along South Great George's Street, Camden Street, Parnell Street, Henry Street, Talbot Street and North Strand, as well as on several of the city's bridges. Some traded from baskets which they laid down on the footpath. In November

Left to right: **Dolly Mangan, Marie Creed and Mary O'Driscoll protest outside Mountjoy Prison at the imprisonment of Tony Gregory and Christy Burke (1986)**

1921, City Magistrates Lupton and Cooper made some suggestions about how they might be treated. They strongly favoured their removal from the main thoroughfares and tried to coax them into the Iveagh Markets, which had vacant space for at least forty stalls.

By the 1980s the situation had changed very little, apart from the appearance of the Silver Cross pram with a breadboard slung across it. Local businesses took exception to hawkers outside their premises and in response the Garda Síochána began to deploy 'snatch squads'. Every day traders could be seen dashing down Henry Street. The unlucky ones were rounded up and carted off to Store Street or Fitzgibbon Street garda stations. For a woman trying to feed a family, the prospect of an entire day spent in a cell, coupled with the confiscation of her goods, was a difficult cross to bear.

Those who remained faced arrest, but they found strong advocates in Independent TD Tony Gregory and Councillor Christy Burke. Later, both men would recall that they seemed to spend most of their time at police stations, pleading on the women's behalf. In 1984, 600 prosecutions were brought against the traders. It angered the two men that these women were being prevented from making a living when more pressing social problems seemed to go unchecked.

Independent TD Tony Gregory and Dolly Mangan (1986).
(Courtesy of Derek Speirs)

Despite their intervention, police fines increased and many of the more transient traders began to disappear from the area. The turning point came in March 1985, when two arrests were made on Henry Street for breaches of the illegal trading act. A large group of traders made their way up to the front of the GPO on Lower O'Connell Street to protest. They blocked traffic and the Gardaí were drafted in from nearby stations to deal with the situation. There were violent confrontations when they refused to move, culminating in a baton charge. Christy Burke would later recall:

> We were arrested, myself and Tony Gregory and a few of the women, and
> I remember we were put into a van but we were coming up O'Connell
> Street and the van doors got booted open and myself and Gregory jumped,
> ran – I got caught; he got away – he was arrested again an hour later.[13]

That October the two men were brought before the Dublin District Court, along with a number of the street traders, bound to keep the peace for six months and fined. They refused to pay and were sentenced to two weeks in prison in January 1986. Speaking outside the district courthouse, Gregory was unequivocal. 'You have a constitutional right to earn a living … to rear your families and to provide for your families and if we have to take a constitutional case to win this issue, we'll do it. We're going to take it right to the bitter end.'[14] The traders did not let them languish in a prison cell for long. They took their prams and their placards and marched up to Mountjoy. Their anthem was 'Stand by your Pram'. The protest and the embarrassment it caused forced a change. As a result, many transient pitches on Cole's Lane, Marlborough Street and O'Connell Bridge have since been regularised.

Independent TD Tony Gregory on his release from Mountjoy Prison, 7 February 1986.
(Courtesy of Matt Kavanagh of The Irish Times*)*

Traders had to eke out a living wherever they could. This photograph was taken outside 16 Upper Liffey Street. *(RSAI lantern slide 17:77, courtesy of the Royal Society of Antiquaries of Ireland)*

Darkest Dublin:
the harsher side of market life

Whitelaw's census of St Mary's Parish, taken in 1798, shows that excluding Henry and Great Britain Streets, 2,553 people lived in the Moore Street district. With an average of thirteen people per house, the area was overcrowded. The highest number of inhabitants could be found in Little Denmark Street and Cole's Lane.[15]

A careful comparison between this census and that of 1911 is revealing. Superficially it would seem that there was little real change in the overall population. However, when the inhabitants are tallied on a street by street basis, a trend emerges. The residential populations of Henry Street and Moore Street, which stood at 571 and 683 prior to the Act of Union, had fallen to just 171 and 363 by 1911 – a clear indication of the newfound commercial status of those thoroughfares. The picture for the market interior was almost the exact opposite. There, the numbers nearly doubled over a century as people began to cram into houses on the laneways.

Anglesea Market *c.* 1930. Note the impressive granite flags with channels for rainwater drain-off. *(Courtesy of Terry Fagan)*

By the early nineteenth century, Moore Street and its surrounding district were home to the largest number of traders in the city, with seventy-nine stalls spread throughout the narrow lanes and thoroughfares. One account of Rotunda Market complimented it for the availability of 'cheap and excellent meat', but lamented that the stalls were often:

> placed in low and confined situations – either blocking up the passages of streets or lanes, or surrounded by high houses where the free passage of air is prevented … there are no public slaughterhouses and the animals are killed behind the stalls or in the very place where the meat is sold, and the accumulation of ordure and offal in the market is sometimes highly offensive.[16]

The Dublin Builder of 15 March 1861 painted a similar picture of the area, noting the 'decayed vegetables, fish entrails, sawdust, sweepings from the stalls', not just in the Moore Street area, but also in Pill Lane, William Street and D'Olier Street. The article contrasted this with the public markets in Liverpool and Manchester, where there was an 'abundance of ventilation, water, and scrupulous cleanliness'.[17]

By then a large number of city-centre slaughterhouses and dairy yards were in operation, but they had long been recognised as a public nuisance. Jacinta Prunty notes that of the ninety-nine slaughterhouses registered with Dublin Corporation in 1879, the highest concentration could be found in the most congested parts of the city.[18] Of those in the Moore Street area, Seán O'Casey recalled:

> The lane, stretching from Cole's Lane at one end, to Moore Street at the other, was half filled with cattle, lowing in a frightened way; some of them trying to steal or run away from the murky entrances of the slaughterhouses, slipping madly, sometimes in the slime of their own dung that pooled the cobble-stones. There was a heavy reek in the air of filth and decaying blood scattered over the yards, and heaps of offal lay about watched by a restless herd of ragged women and youngsters, taking their chance to dive in and snatch a piece of liver or green-slimed guts to carry home as a feast for the favoured.[19]

Cole's Lane, *c.* 1900. The barefoot children are particularly striking in this image. *(Reproduced by permission of the Royal Society of Antiquaries of Ireland)*

In an attempt to address the situation, Dublin Corporation established its own slaughterhouse, from which it hoped to raise enough funds to provide local services such as street cleaning, but local people preferred to use their own facilities, which were cheaper.

City Analyst Sir Charles Cameron was a frequent visitor to the area. On 14 June 1870, he attended the scene of a cattle slaughter at Sampson's Lane in which he determined the meat to be unfit for human consumption on account of it not having been bled. The carcasses were later transported to Dublin Zoo for the use of the animals.[20]

On 1 December 1872, *The Freeman's Journal* reported on the case of Francis Richardson of Riddall's Row, whom it described as a 'carrion trafficker'. He appeared in court to answer a complaint made by Mr Webb, Inspector of Markets, for having produced semi-putrid beef for sale. Dr Cameron confirmed that it was badly diseased 'and utterly unfit for human food'. Richardson was sentenced to three months' hard labour as a deterrent to others.

During the summer the traders were often plagued by flies and other insects, and tenement hallways in the neighbourhood were painted with a strong mixture of lime and water called 'red raddle' in an attempt to deter these pests. Some areas, such as the 'bone yard' just off the Lime Yard, swam with fly larvae or 'chandlers'. Rats were also a constant nuisance. Many of the local men kept terriers and Jack Russells, which helped to curb their numbers. In 1939 the local men formed an anti-rat association and pooled their resources to call in exterminators. Seamus Marken (aged eighty-three) recalls:

> We used to hunt rats around the Lime Yard at night for sport. There was a street light at one end; we started by breaking that. Then all the rats would come. The place would be swarming with them once it was dark. When kennel clubs started sporting terrier dogs, they used to come to us to 'blood' them. My uncle had a big barrel in the back. There was only him and I in on it. We would put a rat into the barrel. You got your dog and put him in on top of that. Now if the dog was a real terrier, he'd kill him. That meant your dog was blooded. We charged the clubs 10s for that. It was big money.[21]

The slaughterhouse men were particularly accommodating to those who bred dogs for fighting, allowing them to take away waste parts such as sheep's reeds (the fourth stomach) or skull bones. My father (aged seventy-two) recalls that when he was a boy living near the market area, they used to place bets on how many rats a dog might kill in a barrel. During the week, these dogs could be found nosing for scraps around the various stalls and shops.[22]

By the mid nineteenth century, many of the houses in the market area had fallen into dereliction. Prohibition orders were occasionally made by the authorities. In 1847 a doctor from Sackville Court wrote a long letter to *The Freeman's Journal*, calling attention to 'that portion of the city known as Cole's Lane market, with its adjoining avenues' all of which were in an 'unprecedented state of filth'.[23] In 1866 the corporation's sanitary officers summoned a large number of residents from Horseman's Row, Great Britain Street, Jervis Lane and Mason's Market under the Public Health Act for 'allowing' their premises to become run down. They noted the absence of water closets, ash pits and proper sewerage. At an enquiry held at Capel Street police court on 5 October, Mr Newman, the assistant corporation engineer, testified that:

> In some instances, such as in the houses in Horseman's Row … there was no room for the erection of water closets, unless actually in the rooms in which the inhabitants lived, his worship stated it as his conviction that the houses should be shut up or destroyed.[24]

In October 1875 No. 22 Riddall's Row collapsed. Miraculously, nobody was injured in the incident.[25] In May 1884 orders were once again made prohibiting the use of eight houses in Mason's Market.[26] A further six were identified as dangerous in Rotunda Market in 1886, but in five of these cases the owners were given time to rectify the situation.[27]

Condemned buildings were to be boarded up, but sometimes violence broke out between locals who lived there and the authorities who tried to enforce this measure. In February 1920 a crowd of about 200 strong, led by J. W. Larkin, secretary of the Dublin Tenants' Association, attempted to prevent a contractor from erecting a hoarding around No. 28 Riddall's Row. During the incident, Larkin was said to have pulled a plank out of the contractor's hand.[28]

Norfolk Market *c.* 1900.
*(Reproduced by permission of the Royal
Society of Antiquaries of Ireland)*

Inevitably, many of the buildings were abandoned. They became temporary shelters for stall equipment or were used as playgrounds for local children. Seamus Marken recalls one abandoned tenement in Little Denmark Street:

> People had pulled up the floorboards for firewood. Now, at the back of it, there was a huge waste ground called the 'Ouler' where there had been buildings of some kind, but in my day it was all flattened. We used to go and dig holes in it, make trenches and play war. When we'd be chased by the police for playing football or jeering them, we used to run like hell through the markets. Once we got across the Ouler, we'd go through the tenement. We had to sort of hug the wall with one foot on a joist. Then we were out into Denmark Street, Chapel Lane and away. Most policemen might chase you as far as there, but they wouldn't bother going any further. One time, a copper thought he was good so he kept on chasing us. Of course, we ran through the building as usual. He ran after us but fell on the joists; he started screaming. We had to get a man in Denmark Street to call an ambulance and take him away.[29]

In 1902 a semi-derelict house in Moore Lane collapsed, trapping a twelve-year-old boy inside. The local fire brigade dug for seven hours, but were unable to locate his remains. It was only when the corporation workmen moved in to remove the debris that his body was finally discovered lying under a pile of masonry.[30]

Fire was another ever-present hazard in the cramped confines of the narrow market streets, particularly in laneways where piles of rubbish accumulated. During the 1880s the corporation paid for two men and a horse to clean it away on a daily basis, but by the early 1900s this arrangement had lapsed and cleaning was only performed on Sundays.

In 1940 there was a Dublin Corporation strike – a significant problem for the area's poulterers, fishmongers and butchers, who accumulated offal behind their stalls every day. Other traders tried to do the best they could by sweeping up rotten fruit, cabbage leaves and other debris, and dumping it into the nearby alleys. One local in Sampson's Lane ended up with a pile of market rubbish about two feet deep outside their house. When they attempted to burn it, they found themselves threatened by corporation workers on the basis that it would not help the workers' cause.

In November 1837 a blaze broke out in a chemist's in Off (Moore) Lane, claiming the lives of three women who were unable to break through the barred windows upstairs.[31] In 1846 a further three houses burned down in Moore Street. In September 1900 a man at work in his home in Rotunda Market was burned to death when his oil lamp fell and his shirt sleeve caught fire.[32] In January 1915 a blaze was discovered in an oil store in Sampson's Lane. On arrival, the fire service encountered the following:

> A large cask of petroleum flowing down the channel of the laneway, past the back of several of the large shops in Henry Street … Captain Purcell had two lines of hose laid down, and his men extinguished the fire in thirty-five minutes, before it had spread to any of the adjoining buildings. This, however, was not the end of the fire. Two hours later the Brigade was again summoned to the same building to put out another fire, which had broken out in a hayloft.[33]

Despite the dangers, locals could not do without heat, particularly during the cold months. During the winter of 1882, they lit a bonfire on Great Britain (Parnell) Street which consisted of sticks, wood shavings, old straw bedding and everything within their reach: 'The fire burned brightly and briskly to their heart's content, round which they gathered in conviviality to give themselves a good toasting away from the cold, which they must have fully experienced in their scantily clothed bodies and shoeless feet.'[34]

Problems of sanitation, fire and disease were a product of overcrowding. The people of Moore Street tried to take matters into their own hands by destroying their own rubbish, running makeshift water pipes off the main supply and hiring rat catchers, but it would take a concerted effort by the city authorities to put things right. It is a sobering thought that the experiences of the nineteenth-century market dwellers were not all that different to those of their mid-twentieth-century counterparts and that darkest Dublin is still within living memory.

A picture of Henry Street taken by Keogh Brothers in the aftermath of the Rising. *(Courtesy of the National Library of Ireland)*

The 1916 Rising: a ringside view

The gloom was gathering on a Friday evening when the remaining men holed up in Dublin's General Post Office (GPO) were ordered into the main hall. They were a defiant but battle-weary group. Overhead, the building was now on fire, unable to cope with a relentless bombardment of incendiary shells.

Just five days earlier, the mood had been more optimistic when a group of Irish Volunteers and 200 soldiers of the Irish Citizen Army marched out from nearby Beresford Place, outside Liberty Hall, under the leadership of Patrick Pearse, James Connolly and Joseph Plunkett. With the city on holiday for Easter Monday, it was relatively easy for them to seize possession of the newly renovated GPO.

The leaders of the resistance were already well known to many of those who lived in the local area. Locals often good-naturedly jeered the Volunteers when they marched past on parade, and Connolly himself had once shopped for a table in Cole's Lane Market.[35] Countess Markievicz, who was to occupy the Royal College of Surgeons building in St Stephen's Green, was known as 'Madame' by the traders on Moore Street, and the traders in turn would become 'Madame's wans'.[36]

Across the city, the rebel divisions received support from market men. Some were

Flowersellers at Nelson's pillar, *c.* 1900. These were among the first to evacuate O'Connell Street on Easter Monday 1916.
(Courtesy of the O'Leary family)

members of the Irish Citizen Army. Others were Irish Volunteers. They included Tom McEvoy from Sampson's Lane as well as four of the sons of poulterer Christopher Flanagan from No. 30½ Moore Street. One of these lads would later meet his death on the barricades at Church Street.[37] Thomas Munroe, a labourer named Martin Foy and a caretaker named Patrick Hughes hailed from Nos 7, 21 and 30 Little Denmark Street respectively. Other locals who took part included Patrick Murray from Chapel Lane, a hairdresser from Cole's Lane named John Farmer and over a dozen men from Parnell Street, most of whom were shop assistants or bar workers.[38]

Fifty-eight-year-old street trader Maggie Wade recalled the scene at Nelson's Pillar. 'The men in green disarmed the soldiers in khaki,' she later told a reporter. 'The bullets were flying round the flowers and we ran for our lives. We were not back at the pitch until next Saturday.'[39] Within hours of the rebels seizing the GPO, the scene in the adjacent area had become chaotic: 'At Moore Street corner, the public houses were fast being sold out. One met drunken men and women frequently … drapery shops, jewellers, sweet and tobacco shops, spirit grocers in the vicinity of the provisional government's headquarters, had all been, or were being looted.'[40]

This situation was made worse by the closure of the police station on Henry Street. When three policemen were shot on the first day of the fighting, the Police Commissioner took his men off the streets. In their absence, the looters had a field day. They lit a bonfire near the Parnell Monument, and in Moore Lane they broke into Keeley's Stores and stole a number of handcarts, piling them with stolen goods until they were overflowing. 'Tattered barefoot kids – gorged on sweets – pelted one another with packets of tea and sugar, footballing tins of preserves into the roadway, to the delight of the grinning shawled auld ones.'[41] One enterprising Moore Street resident ambushed looters with a toy gun; they took it to be real and relinquished

British Army barricade at the top of Moore Street. Note the improvised use of a butcher's block. *(From Daily Sketch postcard for Eason & Sons, courtesy of Theeasterrising.eu)*

their haul. Such efforts were not enough to stem the tide, however. Gorman's shop at No. 15 was denuded of its '2,000 Woodbine cigarettes, 500 Players, 300 Gold Flake and 700 Park Drive', while Cogan's at Nos 10–12 lost its entire stock-in-trade to the value of £780.[42] At Nos 11, 22 and 23 Moore Street, looters spirited away tins of biscuits, skipper sardines, John West salmon and fruit, as well as Oxo cubes, packets of butter, pickles and jam. They did not forget to take the cutlery with which to eat their bounty.[43]

Although taken initially by surprise, the authorities soon rallied, and concerted efforts were made to bring in British Army troops. Arriving in Parnell Street, the

33 Little Denmark Street – headquarters of the Dublin Typographical Provident Society. During Easter Week, it housed British Army troops.
(Courtesy of Tom Bridgeman)

soldiers scouted for vantage points from which to lay siege to the GPO. At first, they could not be sure of all of the rebel positions. Suspicious that one house was harbouring enemy troops, they prepared to lay down machine-gun fire until one of their colleagues pleaded with them to hold fire. He had family members living there and asked for permission to get them to safety first.[44]

At the same time, a number of buildings on Little Denmark Street were also occupied by the British Army. These included the Marine Stores at No. 18 and the

Typographical Provident Society – an imposing four-storey building whose top windows afforded an excellent view of the Henry and Liffey Street junction.[45]

Once the soldiers had taken up their positions, the men in the GPO were unable to engage in a great deal of direct fighting. On Tuesday evening the rebels received reinforcements, when the garrisons that had occupied Annesley Bridge and Fairview arrived. That night, the Fairview men were sent to erect barricades on Henry Street at either side of the Moore Street opening, but they came into conflict with looters who were trying to take away furniture and other large items.

By Wednesday evening the rebels had managed to bore through a number of houses on Henry Street, all the way to the Coliseum Theatre (No. 24). McDowell's Jewellers at No. 27 had been taken at an early stage, but the new post was an important one as it commanded the approach from Moore Street. The theatre, newly built, afforded another key advantage in that it would be much more difficult to destroy. The stairs, landings and passages were built from concrete, reinforced with expanded metal and rolled steel joists. The circle and gallery were also carried by a framework of steel, protected by asbestos. A large lantern light in the roof over the stage was designed to have automatic opening sides so that, in the event of a fire, smoke and flames would be drawn away from the proscenium opening. There was also an ample number of hydrants and sprinkler systems.[46]

As the week dragged on, local people began to starve in their houses. Some were helped by the British Army. Molly Darcy recalled to her grandson, Bill Cullen, that 'the soldiers gave us some of their rations … Odd lumps of hard meat to chew on but it kept us going.'[47] Those who were able to venture outside made a rush on the Parnell Street bakeries, where loaves were being sold for 4*d*, a halfpenny below their usual price. In the absence of the police, the military were obliged to try to maintain law and order. Paddy Ormsby (aged seventy-nine) recalls:

> My grandmother was looking for bread for to feed the kids; she went down with a pillowcase (they used to use them when they'd be going to Kennedy's bakery to throw the bread in it); the British soldiers stopped her and said, 'Where's your Fenian bastard of a husband?' My grandmother said, 'Where you should be.' 'And where should we be?' they asked her. 'Out in the Dardanelles,' she says, 'he's in the army.' That was enough for

them. They took her to the bakery, filled up her pillowslip with bread and sent her on her way.[48]

The fruit and vegetable market at Halston Street remained closed for ten days. During that time, one trader lost to over-ripening three barrels of apples, ten and a half cases of lemons and ninety bunches of bananas. Looters managed to get into sheds belonging to Ted Castle McCormick at Sir John Rogerson's Quay, where they carted away a staggering twenty-eight bags of Egyptian onions.[49]

With Moore Street market closed, many Dubliners cycled into the rural hinterland of the city to buy milk, butter, meat and eggs from small farmers. In other places, the army broke open stores and warehouses in order to feed civilians.

Some locals wanted to help the men holed up in the post office. 'Sure they must be starving,' said Kate Leonard, a trader from Halston Street. 'There's nothing in that GPO only stamps.' She made up a parcel of apples for them. The general feeling was one of animosity, however, particularly from local women, some of whom worried that the Rising would prevent their receipt of government-funded 'separation money' – paid to them because they had sons and husbands away fighting in the British Army. Indeed, so many had joined the British Army that the Typographical Provident Society on Little Denmark Street was obliged to replace its male operators with women for the duration of the war.

On Wednesday the city fire department led by Captain Purcell braved the gunfire to tackle a blaze that broke out in Williams' Stores in Sampson's Lane. They arrived to find the stores being looted, and although the building was saved, its contents were not.

The following afternoon, James Connolly sent a party of men to occupy a local tailoring firm called the Henry Street Warehouse, but soon transferred them to O'Neill's at the corner of Upper Liffey Street, where they would remain until after the surrender that Saturday. The shop commanded the Mary Street and Little Denmark Street approaches to Henry Street, in particular the army-held Typographical Provident Society. Diarmuid Lynch recalled that, 'a little later this locality was reconnoitred by an enemy armoured car; our men could only regret their lack of suitable armament to deal effectively with it'.[50]

Nevertheless, the Volunteers must not have been completely impotent from that position. After one firefight, a British soldier staggered into Margaret Kennerk's small grocery shop at No. 23 Little Denmark Street. He died in her arms on the shop floor, insisting that he was a Catholic and that he wanted a priest.[51] Another soldier was dragged to safety at No. 47B Moore Street, Christy O'Leary's butcher shop.[52]

By Thursday the GPO was under heavy artillery bombardment and uncontrolled fires were taking a heavy toll on buildings along Henry Street, Moore Street and Cole's Lane. From time to time, ambulances could be seen making the perilous journey towards Jervis Street Hospital. The crews had huge difficulty trying to persuade the British Army soldiers to allow them to remove the dead or injured. In most instances, they were left lying on the street. That same day, a companion of rebel chaplain Father John Flanagan was shot as he made his way up Moore Street. Flanagan 'administered the last rites' and, afterwards, 'two courageous lads bore the dying man to Jervis St Hospital in a handcart'.[53]

During the early part of Easter Week, the British Army had no defensive fortifications, but they still managed to sweep the main streets of the market with machine-gun fire, perhaps in an effort to deter people from attempting to approach the GPO.[54] Later, they assembled three barricades – one at the Parnell Street end of Little Denmark Street, another at Moore Lane and a third at Moore Street. The latter was made from butchers' blocks, crates and barrels as well as a pony van which was most likely turned on its side. This belonged to Mrs Kelly from Nos 24 and 25 Moore Street.[55]

On Cole's Lane eleven-year-old Tom Mooney had a lucky escape as he stood at his hall door.[56] His neighbour was not so fortunate: he was shot dead as he attempted to fetch a doctor for his wife.[57] A woman near Riddall's Row was also fatally wounded as she crouched near her bedroom window, while her neighbour died when he stood up to light his pipe. John Murphy, a sixty-year-old justice of the peace and chairman of the Rathdown Rural District Council, from 42 Henry Street, was shot and killed as he attempted to leave for his sister's home.[58] Many local people were taken to nearby Jervis Street Hospital, which was saved from being burned by the Trojan efforts of the fire service.

The Dillon family, who owned a grocer's called 'The Flag' at Nos 6 and 8 towards the Henry Street end of Moore Street, began to fear for their safety. When Mr Dillon

walked up to the barricade, he was told curtly that 'if he dared to proceed another step, he would be shot'.[59] His orders were to return to his home and stay there. Reluctantly he obeyed, but by Friday the firing outside had become so intense that he decided to make another attempt. He and his family were able to escape through the garden and stores to No. 6 and into the workshop, where they stayed all night until 5 a.m. on the morning of Saturday 29 April.

Outside, the early pre-dawn sky was lit in amber and yellow as a blaze razed the roof of the nearby GPO. In horror, the Dillons noticed that one of the barricades across Henry Street had ignited, setting fire to a neighbouring dairy belonging to Miss Morris. It was now burning uncontrollably. Through a spyglass, Captain Purcell of the fire brigade could also see what was happening, but was unable to do anything about it.

Hemmed in, the family were left with little choice but to run for the opposite side of the street. Together with the residents of No. 5, they left in an orderly crowd, mostly women and children under the protection of white flags. The little party had almost reached the house across the street when a shot rang out from the Parnell Street barricade, catching Mr Dillon in the throat. He was killed instantly. The rest of the party managed to get to relative safety.

Meanwhile, fearing that the adjacent chemist shop would catch fire, the Doyle and McDonagh families – tenants of No. 16 – attempted to reach the refuge of a neighbouring house. Mr Doyle and his wife were both shot, but were pulled to safety by the O'Carroll family at No. 49. Inside, a crowd of people huddled together for safety. Eventually, a neighbour named Gorman slipped through the slaughterhouses to obtain a temporary ceasefire. On his return, preparations were made to leave the house: 'Mrs O'Carroll, with a white sheet attached to a long-caned duster, along with her husband and three children headed the party. Mr Doyle was carried in a blanket, followed by his wobbling wife supporting her wounded leg with an umbrella.'[60]

By now the fire had spread to the west side of Moore Street. With incredible courage, Miss Morris left her place of shelter. In open daylight, she walked towards the military barricade waving a white flag. She told the British officers that somewhere in a house down the street crouched a defenceless group of men, women and children. 'For God's sake, let them out,' she pleaded. Her request was flatly denied. Refusing to yield, she knelt on the cobbles until the senior officer relented and gave permission for the crowd of people to be evacuated across the barricade. Their one condition was that the men be taken prisoner with Morris as a hostage.

The crowd of people, broken and dispirited, must have made a sorry spectacle as they walked towards the barricade. A number of local businesses had been pressed into service as temporary shelters for local civilians. These included the looted Home and Colonial Stores (just behind the British Army barricade on the corner of Moore Street), Harold's Cross Laundry and the Rotunda Hospital. The women and children were locked into a tenement house facing Moore Street. Miss Dillon later recalled that all the while, 'we saw our property, 6 and 6½, Moore Street, reduced to a heap of burning ruins, and my father's corpse lying on the pavement opposite'.[61]

At about eight o'clock on Friday evening, 28 April 1916, one of the final chapters of the Rising took place. The remaining men in the GPO were summoned by Patrick Pearse. Taking as much food and ammunition as they could carry, they were ordered to strike out for Williams & Woods' factory building on Parnell Street. Many didn't know where the factory was. Confusion reigned. As they were ordered to unload their weapons, one man injured himself in the foot with a shotgun.[62]

They left the building in three main stages. The first group, led by one of the founding members of the Irish Volunteers, Michael Joseph O'Rahilly (The O'Rahilly), struck out from the shell-damaged and burning GPO. He and his small party of men hoped to create a diversion at the nearby Moore and Parnell Street barricade. By so doing, they would help the remainder of the escape party to reach the new headquarters.

Travelling via Henry Place, they emerged onto Moore Street. Coming under fire, The O'Rahilly was injured, but one of his party – a twenty-eight-year-old man named Henry Coyle – helped him to safety before being fatally wounded himself. As the men ran across Moore Street towards a looted and burnt factory owned by Williams & Woods in Sampson's Lane, bullets tore into the soft gable wall of No. 55 Moore Street beside them.[63]

With bayonet fixed, The O'Rahilly led his men in a charge up Moore Street – half on the left, the other half on the right. The weapons were woefully inadequate for the task. 'I noticed one man who stepped forward for the charge,' Volunteer Joseph Good recalled. 'He was armed with a shotgun and a bayonet made of … Bessemer steel … a number of these bayonets had been made in Kimmage, but they would have bent against three-ply wood.'[64] When they were within about fifty yards of the enemy line, The O'Rahilly paused in a closed doorway and waited until the burst of gunfire had stopped. Then he resumed the charge with a blow of his whistle. There was a flash of bullet fire. He fell, mortally wounded, but managed to reach the relative safety of Sackville Lane, partly helped by Volunteer Tom Crimmons. Later, the area near the Moore Street barricade would earn the title of 'Dead Man's Corner'.

Earlier, while wounded in Sampson's Lane, The O'Rahilly had written a hurried note to his family. It was scribbled on the back of a letter his son had delivered to the GPO:

> Written after I was shot. Darling Nancy I was shot leading a rush up Moore Street and took refuge in a doorway. While I was there I heard the men pointing out where I was and made a bolt for the laneway I am in now. I got more [than] one bullet I think. Tons and tons of love dearie to you and the boys and to Nell and Anna. It was a good fight anyhow.[65]

Entrance to Moore Street Market, *c.* 1950. It was here that Captain Seán McEntee and his men found refuge during the GPO evacuation. *(Courtesy of the Irish Architectural Archive)*

In a frantic attempt to find help for his stricken leader, Crimmins knocked at the doors of an adjacent fish market and public house, but got no answer.

Meanwhile, Irish Volunteer Captain Seán MacEntee, who had stopped to get his bearings, noticed that some of the men had managed to reach the relative safety of Moore Street Market, a narrow laneway on the left side of Moore Street with a heavy brick entrance. There they were protected from machine-gun fire, but they were still in view of an unseen marksman. MacEntee, who was carrying a shotgun, turned to take aim at a house behind him. He would later recall that as he did so he saw 'the pale, horrified face of a frightened woman' in a window.[66]

He managed to get into the laneway unscathed, but was now separated from the remainder of the GPO evacuees. He and his men opened fire on the British troops, but were soon forced to give up. MacEntee asked one of the Volunteers whether it might be possible to reach Williams & Woods on Parnell Street by another route. 'Yes,' he replied. 'This lane opens on a street which leads to the rear of the factory.' As they emerged onto Cole's Lane, they came under another concentrated burst of fire.

With dusk falling and five of the men wounded, they made their way back to the corner of Riddall's Row, where they found a newly built brick stable. MacEntee describes what happened next:

> In a trice, we had the lock off the door and were in possession. Loopholes were quickly knocked in the walls. Hay was found in abundance and beds were soon made for the wounded. These last were in a sorry plight. One boy had his foot laid open by a bullet, so that from toe to heel, it was a gaping wound.[67]

The wounded were helped by locals who lived in the vicinity of Horseman's Row.[68] Inside the stable lay a meagre store of provisions – a few biscuits, some chocolate and a few jelly squares. The men took up watch.

About half an hour after The O'Rahilly had made his desperate charge, the remainder of the evacuees, including Joseph Plunkett, Michael Collins, Patrick Pearse, Harry Boland and Diarmuid Lynch, also exited the GPO. As they passed the barricade their men had erected on the corner of Moore Street, Plunkett spotted an injured Dublin Fusilier on the other side, moaning for water. He carried him, despite the gunfire, into Henry Place.[69]

At the bend where Henry Place met Moore Lane, the party was exposed to sniper fire coming from the Rotunda Hospital and the bell tower of Findlater's Church. The bullets ricocheted off a white-painted warehouse, giving the rebels the impression that it was under enemy occupation. A squad rushed in, only to realise their mistake.

Under the cover of a hastily erected barricade built from an old cab, a cart and empty crates from a nearby mineral-water factory, the party dashed back into Henry Place. Some tried to break down a door with their rifle butts but failed to realise that the safety catches were off.[70] With three or four of their comrades wounded as a result, they reached a small yard fronting a cottage inhabited by the McKane family. One of the Volunteers attempted to break the door lock, but ended up shooting Mr McKane who was trying to open it from the far side. The baby he was carrying in his arms escaped injury but, disastrously, the bullet passed through one of his shoulders and killed his fifteen-year-old daughter Brigid. The scene was chaotic as a crowd of Volunteers, many of them injured, filled the little yard. In her panic, Mrs McKane ran for a priest, waving a pillowslip as a white flag.[71]

The 'White House' at the junction of Moore Lane and Henry Place. Ricocheting bullets gave rebels the false impression that it housed British Army troops.
(Courtesy of Terry Fagan)

Nurse Elizabeth O'Farrell.
(*Courtesy of Terry Fagan*)

The wounded were attended by nurse Elizabeth O'Farrell and her school friend Julia Grenan. Afterwards, the Volunteers managed to gain access to Cogan's grocery shop at the corner of Moore Street and Henry Place. In the process, they startled Mrs Cogan who was skinning a cooked ham.

A council of war was held in the basement. An eighteen-year-old member of the Fianna named Seán McLoughlin, whose level-headedness during the evacuation had impressed Patrick Pearse, was promoted to commandant general by the wounded James Connolly. Afterwards, Lieutenant Oscar Traynor and a band of men were assigned to tunnel northwards through Moore Street at second-floor level in the direction of Parnell Street. Another party, who had been assigned by Pearse to occupy the rooftops, were obliged to beat a hasty retreat by the oncoming fire.

Of the whole enterprise, Volunteer Seamus Kavanagh later recalled:

> I felt very sorry for the people who lived in these houses. By going into them we were bringing death and destruction to the inhabitants, though we tried to make things as easy as we could. The floors in those houses were not at the same level, so that when we broke through the wall on a landing of one house we often found ourselves a good distance above the floor of the next, and mostly we would find we had burst from a hall or landing into a living or bedroom where frightened people were huddled together wondering what would happen to them.[72]

The route taken by the escaping rebels was tortuous and very painful for the injured Connolly, whose stretcher had to be negotiated up and down, around tight hairpin bends and through awkward openings. 'We spent Friday night barricading all the houses that we occupied by throwing down all the furniture from the rooms,' Eamonn Bulfin recalled. 'One shell hit a house which we had evacuated, down at the lower part of Moore Street, and flattened it out absolutely. It went down like a house of cards.'[73]

By Saturday 29 April they had reached No. 16 – a poultry shop then owned by a family named Plunkett. Meanwhile, the Volunteers continued to burrow along the street. In an attempt to draw the attention of the British, Pearse ordered Frank Henderson to erect a 'mock barricade' across Moore Street towards Sampson's Lane.

Using some ropes, he ran a cart into the middle of Moore Street. He threw out some boxes and sacks filled with hay:

> Immediately the cart appeared, the British opened fire, which was very intense. Amongst the men who fired from the barricade were the late Harry Boland and Tom McGrath, recently deceased. Shots were exchanged for a period, the duration of which I cannot now estimate. At one period during the firing, some kind of a missile fell beside our barricade. I was told afterwards that this was an incendiary bomb which did not explode.[74]

With the help of this diversion, Seán McLoughlin and Seán MacDermott tunnelled through the houses as far as Sackville Lane, where they found the body of The O'Rahilly. As they returned to the relative safety of Plunketts', there was a loud clatter of hooves in the street as some horses were released from a burning stable. Meanwhile, on the other side of the market, Captain MacEntee's men had also begun to bore through the party walls of the houses on Riddall's Row in two directions: towards Moore Street on one side and up towards Parnell Street on the other.

Fires for cooking were lit sparingly in case the chimney smoke might draw sniper fire. From time to time, the men witnessed the attempts of civilians to escape. 'Before it was quite dark I saw an old man come out of a shop on the opposite side of the street,' Seamus Kavanagh recalled. 'No sooner did he appear than a bullet from one of the 18th Royal Irish who were manning a barricade at the end of the street struck him and he fell to the ground.' It soon became apparent to Kavanagh that the man was not dead:

> He remained there all night and for hours it was terrible to hear his cries 'Water, water, give me a drink of water.' It went on for hours until eventually his voice got weaker and finally died away. Later when daylight came a little girl, about 4 or 5 years, came out of the shop and started bawling 'Mammy, mammy, my granddad is dead.' She kept repeating this over and over again. Her mother was inside the door calling her in and afraid to go out herself. She expected to see the child shot at any moment and could do nothing to prevent it.[75]

For those Volunteers who had been injured, the filleting blocks in Hanlon's fishmongers were being used as makeshift beds, but Seán McLoughlin was restless for action. He proposed a plan to scatter turpentine and other fuels from one of the shops across the street and to set fire to it, using the diversion to escape towards Williams & Woods.[76] Alternatively, he suggested that a 'death or glory' squad attack the British barricade from Sackville Lane, giving the main garrison time to break out of the houses on Moore Street, move up Henry Street and link up with Ned Daly's garrison at the Four Courts. This second plan was sanctioned by the rebel leaders although, admittedly, Pearse was worried about the potential civilian casualties. 'I am sorry, I cannot help that,' McLoughlin is said to have replied, 'this is a military operation and I can only make it successful if I don't think about such things.'[77]

On Saturday 29 April, Patrick Pearse saw three civilians shot dead as they carried white flags in the street outside. On that basis he decided that it was time to call a halt to the fight and surrender. McLoughlin was about to charge into Sackville Lane with his squad, but Seán MacDermott found him in time and ordered him to return to HQ. The message of

Christy O'Leary's butcher shop at No. 47B Moore Street, Christmas 1910. A British soldier was dragged to safety here during Easter Week. *Left to right:* Mary Leary, Esther Leary, Jane Leary (née Nibbs), Margaret Leary, John Leary, Margaret Nibbs (née Dixon), Christopher Leary Jnr, Christopher Leary Snr.
(*Courtesy of the O'Leary family*)

A rare glimpse at the first floor interior of No. 16 Moore Street, the Volunteers' last headquarters. The building is now sadly dilapidated. *(Courtesy of Cathal Crimmins, Architect)*

surrender was consigned to Nurse O'Farrell, but before she left the HQ, MacDermott hung a white flag out of a window so that she would not be fired upon.[78]

O'Farrell left Gormans', No. 15 Moore Street, at about 12.45 p.m. The atmosphere was eerily silent. The market, which would normally have been bustling, lay empty, with bodies strewn across the roadway like rag dolls. As she passed Sackville Lane, O'Farrell noticed The O'Rahilly's hat and revolver, but, unaware of his fate, she assumed that he had made it to safety in a nearby house.

Second floor of No. 16 Moore Street.
(Courtesy of Cathal Crimmins, Architect)

When she arrived at the barricade, O'Farrell delivered Pearse's order to an officer. Upon hearing that there were other ladies in the house, he said, 'Take my advice and go down again and bring the other two girls out of it.' He was about to send her back through the barricade when he reconsidered and said, 'However, you had better wait. I suppose this will have to be reported.' She was met by a more senior officer who suspected her of being a spy and had a soldier remove her Red Cross insignia. She was then taken to the National Bank on the corner of Parnell Street and Cavendish Row as a prisoner, and from there to Tom Clarke's shop at 75a Parnell Street, where she met General William Lowe, commander of the British forces in Dublin.[79]

The only term acceptable to Lowe was one of unconditional surrender, and at first he refused to believe that Pearse did not require the use of a stretcher. He released O'Farrell, instructing her to return with an answer from the rebel HQ within half an hour. As she passed, by car, down Moore Street past Sackville Lane, she saw The O'Rahilly's body for the first time.[80]

Lowe's instructions as to how the Republican troops from the GPO should surrender were exacting:

> Carrying a white flag, proceed down Moore Street, turn into Moore Lane and Henry Place, out into Henry Street, and around the pillar to the right-hand side of O'Connell Street. March up to within a hundred yards of the military drawn up at the Parnell Statue, halt, advance five paces and lay down arms.[81]

When he arrived at the barricade, Pearse handed over his sword, canteen and pistol to General Lowe. He signed the document of surrender on a wooden bench that had been used for displaying pickled pig heads.

Not all of the Volunteers were capable of making the march around to O'Connell Street: eighteen were wounded and were put lying on the pavement on Moore Street, the strong mingling with the weak so that they could help each other. William Pearse, brother of Patrick, and Captain Liam Breen were despatched to the opposite side of the market to find Seán MacEntee. Upon hearing that there had been a ceasefire, MacEntee joined the others. Not all of the men were so compliant. One group refused to surrender until Seán MacDermott managed to persuade them to do so.

Meanwhile, the area's civilian population slowly began to venture back outside. The rebels, accorded the honours of war, were allowed to march with their weapons unloaded instead of their hands behind their heads, but the women of Moore Street threw chamber pots and vegetables at them as they passed.[82] That evening, Miss

Dillon was given permission by the officer in charge of the barricade to retrieve her father's corpse from the street. She recalled:

> I went down, accompanied by Miss Morris and the white flag, and when I was just kneeling down, trying to raise him, we were again fired on and very narrowly escaped being shot, as several bullets hit the ground around us. When I returned on the following Wednesday to the house we had lived in, No. 8, I found it completely looted, money, papers, clothes, jewellery, everything was gone, and the walls and roof completely ruined by the fire.

In the aftermath of the fighting, the British Army reported 116 dead, twenty-two of whom were Irishmen. A further 368 were wounded with nine missing. Rebel and civilian casualties ran to 318 with a staggering 2,217 wounded. Although some civilians had been shot intentionally by both sides – either through a refusal to obey orders or out of frustration – the majority were killed or injured by indirect fire. There is certainly a case to be made that more could have been done to evacuate civilians from the market, and in August 1916 this gave rise to some heated debate in the House of Commons. Its members were asked to vote in favour of a considerable sum of money for the support of the army overseas, but, instead, Irish Parliamentary MP Patrick Nugent made calls for compensation for Dublin's civilians.[83]

Some time after his release from the Welsh internment camp at Frongoch, where suspected and known members of the Irish Volunteers were interned after the Rising, Batt O'Connor was sent for by Tom Clarke's wife. Clarke was one of the leaders of the Rising and a signatory of the Proclamation of the Irish Republic. She informed him that the night before his surrender, her husband had written some messages on the walls and door jambs of No. 16 Moore Street. O'Connor agreed to carefully remove and preserve them if possible. On his arrival, he found the following words etched into the plaster: 'We had to evacuate the G.P.O. The boys put up a grand fight, and that fight will save the soul of Ireland.'

Finial detail from No. 55 Moore Street – note the clipped wings. These were most likely shot off during the intense gunfire of Easter Week 1916. (*Courtesy of Matt Walsh* – Irish Independent)

Never failing to pass up an opportunity, street traders
sell fruit to departing British troops on the docks, 1922.
(Courtesy of the National Library of Ireland)

The market recovers after the Rising

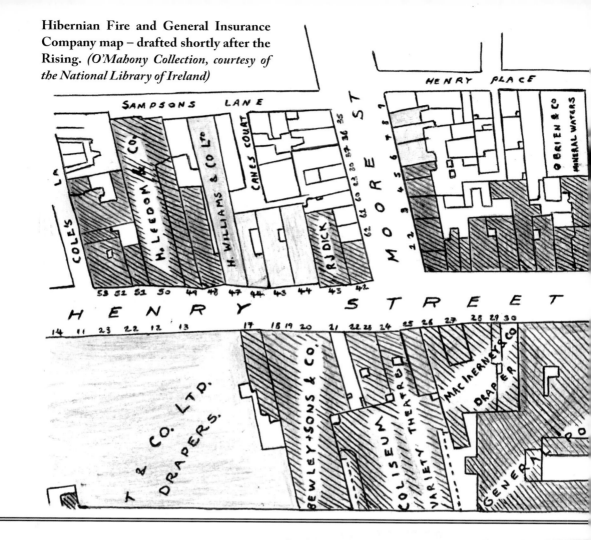

Hibernian Fire and General Insurance Company map – drafted shortly after the Rising. (*O'Mahony Collection, courtesy of the National Library of Ireland*)

The barricades remained on the street for several weeks after the Rising. In an attempt to curb further looting and to deter sightseers, a wooden fence and a night watchman's box were installed at the GPO end of Henry Street.[84] Beyond this, the scene was one of utter devastation. Along the left-hand side of Henry Street from Sackville Street, the buildings had been completely levelled as far as Moore Street, with nothing but piles of broken brick, twisted iron and charred wood left in their place.

Several days after the fighting, Mr Ridgeway, Managing Director of Bewley & Sons, Henry Street, discovered two soldiers still alive, though weak, in the ruins of the Coliseum Theatre, where they had taken refuge during the fighting.

The buildings flanking the entrance to Cole's Lane had all but disappeared. The

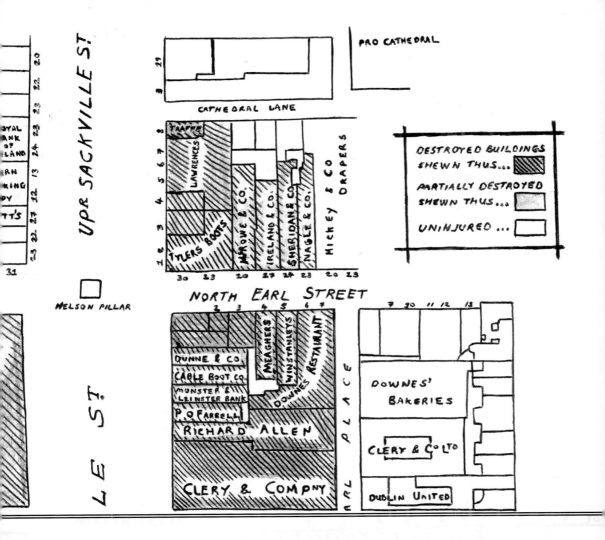

shelves at Samuel's Bazaar, Norton's and Lyons' on Henry Street had been emptied by looters, but Arnotts was still intact. Witnesses described seeing costly pianos being rolled down the street along with suites of furniture, boots, hats and other items of clothing. The police later recovered some of these articles tucked away in basements or in attics across the city.

O'Neill's pub at No. 1 Henry Street was pitted with bullet marks. In total, over thirty premises had been damaged or destroyed. Moore Street fared a little better. There, the damage was mainly confined to ten or so buildings at the Henry Street end. Dunne's pork butchers, which had been saved from a fire in July 1915, was now a smouldering ruin.

A worrying time lay ahead for local traders. In an effort to restore some semblance of normality, the owners of licensed premises were prohibited from opening. Many of the other shops were back in business by 3 May, but some were forced to take up temporary premises in other parts of the city. Having moved to Grafton Street, one firm displayed a burnt piece of shop fitting outside. 'Our Henry Street branch has been transferred to this address,' it read. 'Here it is. The only relic left.'[85] Such relocation was expensive. Business owners were still liable to pay ground rent on their damaged sites, but in effect this meant paying twice – once for the temporary premises and again for the old site.

In an effort to address these and other issues, the Dublin Fire and Property Losses Association was formed on Monday 8 May, under the leadership of businessman William Martin Murphy. Its committee invited local property owners to submit claims for damaged property, with the government agreeing to indemnify the losses. Such governance proved essential. Some insurers, such as Commercial Union, were already trying to claim that their policies did not cover plate glass damaged by 'war or invasion'.[86] On 23 June Ellen Gorman of No. 15 Moore Street read the association's newspaper advertisement for the first time and wrote to the secretary:

> Dear Sir, I see by today's *Independent* that you have under consideration the claims of those who have suffered loss of property during the recent disturbance and as I have made no claim as yet, I beg to ask if you would kindly send me a form of claim to fill up for the loss sustained owing to my shop being looted.[87]

In total almost sixty claims were lodged by market traders. Over half came from Moore Street, with the remainder pertaining to buildings in the adjoining streets. Soon almost all of the city's available builders were employed in clearing away the debris – an unexpected boon considering the depressed state of the construction industry.

Some local property owners had come through Easter Week relatively unscathed. Others, such as Samuel Corbett of Nos 14 and 15 Horseman's Row, had more significant issues to contend with. Contractors' invoices listed damage to his roofs and walls, hall doors and shop shutters. No. 23 Cole's Lane, which belonged to clothes dealer Joseph Durkin, required thirteen new frames of glass, two shutters,

Ruins of the Coliseum Theatre on Henry Street after the fighting.
(Courtesy of the National Library of Ireland)

a door lock and a rainwater pipe – a result of 'firing of cannon immediately outside premises, by rifle fire and by bayonet'.[88]

None of the sites were fenced over with hoarding. This caused at least one business owner (a milliner from 16 Mary Street) to write a letter of complaint to the Chief Commissioner of the Dublin Metropolitan Police. He claimed that he had been injured by stones thrown by gangs of youths who continued to gather 'though the proclamation says they should not do so'. A further gripe was that they tended to put 'their dirty backs against door fronts newly-painted'.[89]

As life returned to the area, some businesses were obliged to reopen under new management due to the death of the previous owner during the Rising. One such was the spirit grocer's at No. 57 Moore Street.[90] Others reopened in temporary structures. These were little more than one-storey shacks, but with their timber uprights and external cladding of galvanised iron or cement plaster, they served a

IMPORTANT SALE OF FIRST-CLASS MODERN LICENSED PREMISES
(Re-built after 1916)
"GRAINGERS"
1 & 2 MOORE STREET, DUBLIN
(CORNER OF HENRY STREET)

FOR AUCTION ON THURSDAY, 29th SEPTEMBER, at 3 p.m.
(UNLESS PREVIOUSLY SOLD)

AT OUR SALEROOMS, LOWER MERRION STREET, DUBLIN

THIS IS UNDOUBTEDLY ONE OF THE FINEST AND MOST IMPOSING LICENSED HOUSES IN THE CITY OF DUBLIN. RE-BUILT AFTER 1916 AND HELD FOREVER, IT CAN BE DESCRIBED AS A PRACTICALLY NEW BUILDING.

THESE PREMISES OCCUPY A MAGNIFICENT TRADING POSITION IN THE VERY HEART OF DUBLIN, IMMEDIATELY ADJACENT TO NELSON PILLAR AND O'CONNELL STREET AND A FEW YARDS FROM THE G.P.O. DAY AFTER DAY THERE IS A GREATER CONCENTRATION OF PEOPLE IN THE VICINITY OF THIS BUSINESS HOUSE, THAN IN ANY OTHER PART OF IRELAND.

AS CAN BE SEEN FROM THE CERTIFIED FIGURES, IT ENJOYS A VERY LARGE AND REMUNERATIVE TRADE.

ACCOMMODATION: Ground Floor: With Central Heating contains large, well-designed, easily-worked Public Bar with fitted wall seating and Bar Tables. Lounge with fitted wall seating and Bar Tables. Gentlemen's Toilets downstairs.

First Floor: Attractive modern Lounge Bar with expensive fitted wall seating. Ladies' Toilet. Store Room with sink, hot press (Immersion Heater). Small Office.

Lofty dry cellars with lift:

THE LIVING ACCOMMODATION COMPRISES: 5 Rooms (3 with hand basins—h. and c.), Bathroom with Shower, Hand basin and w.c. Held for ever subject to £76-19-8 p.a. R.V. £175.

Nos 1 and 2 Moore Street. These premises were among the first to be rebuilt after the Rising. *(Courtesy of the* Irish Press*)*

purpose until more permanent work could be done. Two businesses that reopened temporarily like this were McDowell's Jeweller's at No. 27 and Messrs Marks & Co., who ran a 'Penny Bazaar', at No. 37 Henry Street. The following description of Marks appeared in the *Irish Builder*:

> The structure will be roofed in by timber trusses, covered externally with asphalt. The floors of the shop, stores and rear are to be carried on timber posts from the basement level. The front of the bazaar will be enclosed by folding doors on either side with moveable shutters in the centre. A heavy fascia board is to be put on which will help to mask the ugly outline of the rake of the roof. Light and ventilation will be obtained from the roof.[91]

In other parts of the market, traders were keen to rebuild straight away. By early July, the debris had been removed from Nos 1 and 2 Moore Street, trenches opened and foundations put in.

Contractors' invoices were carefully retained until the Fire and Property Losses Association had a chance to see them. In most cases, compensation awarded by the assessors was fair, albeit falling slightly short of what the owner listed on the claim form. In the case of Thomas Cogan, whose shops at Nos 10 and 12 Moore Street had been looted, no allowance was made for a £7 sewing machine. Similarly, an invoice submitted by Elias Eliassoff of No. 18 Little Denmark Street was struck out on the basis that 'the damage is so trivial in the front portion that the claimant has been able himself to repair it'. In November 1916 Mary Plunkett, whose shop at No. 16 Moore Street became the last headquarters of the rebellion, tried to claim for an outside electric lamp, child's cot, drawing-room table and four linen sheets, but her submission was deemed ineligible on the basis that she had not met the 12 August deadline.[92]

The case of Francis Fee from No. 59 Moore Street was particularly difficult. Shortly after the Rising, he had a temporary roof put on his fire-damaged building. The roof cost £40, but the Association refused to pay, leaving him out of pocket. Fee's architect wrote on 4 August:

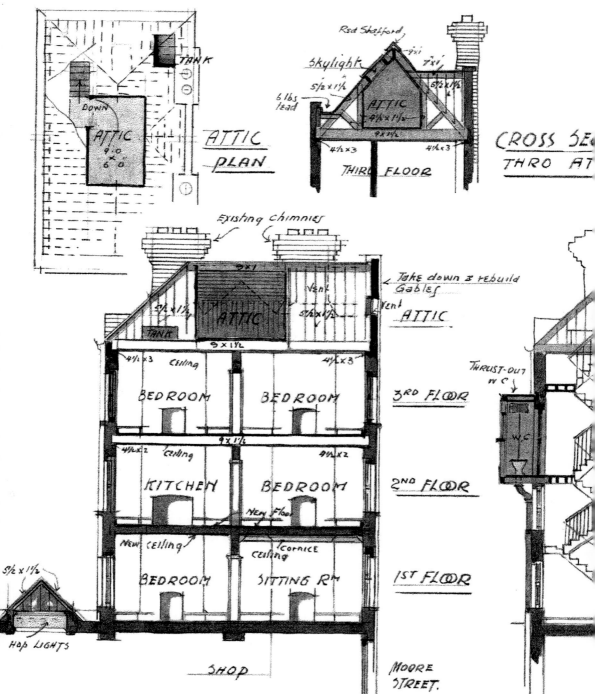

Architectural drawing for Francis Fee of No. 59 Moore Street by J. A. Mandeville.
The shaded areas mark the extent of fire damage caused during Easter Week .
(NAI Property Losses [Ireland] Committee, 1916, File 4633, 3/083/11)

In the interest of my Client, I think it is only fair I should point out that the plans which I lodged with you have not been submitted to, or approved of by the city authorities ... [D]irectly after the rebellion, they notified Mr Fee that his premises were in a dangerous condition [and] may insist on more of the superstructure being taken down, and so put us to further expense, in which case Mr Fee's claim will have to be increased by the value of such requirements of the city authorities.[93]

Along the street, several chimney stacks had toppled over and the cobbles were littered with slates shaken loose by the constant vibration of heavy machine-gun fire. This exposed interior walls to rain damage and added to the rebuilding costs.[94]

Taking stock of events from an architectural perspective, the *Irish Builder* of 13 May 1916 lamented that:

If anything like modern fire-resisting construction had existed, even here and there, the fire might have been stayed and limited to sections; had the steel work been protected by concrete casing, many walls would today be standing and whole sections might possibly have been cut off from the fire.

The city's architects took note. Many of the new buildings incorporated steel joists on stanchions to carry the upper stories as well as concrete floors and piers built of fire brick. The buildings were then clad in red-brick and limestone dressings, with elegant new shop sashes and polished hardwood doors fitted at ground-floor level.

When the leaders of the Rising were executed at Kilmainham, public sympathy began to shift in favour of the Volunteers in prison. These included ordinary men from the market such as Patrick Hughes, a forty-five-year-old caretaker from No. 30 Little Denmark Street, first arrested in September 1915 and charged with the theft of a Lee-Enfield Rifle from a soldier. Later, the police raided his home, where they discovered a Mauser rifle.[95] His release on probation allowed him to take part in the events of Easter Week. From his bunk in Frongoch, Hughes decided to apply for temporary Christmas release. The reason he gave was that his fifteen-year-old daughter Kathleen was seriously ill at home, but when Inspector Love of the Dublin Metropolitan Police was sent to investigate, he found that the girl had nothing more than influenza. 'She is not confined to bed or seriously ill,' he wrote, 'and was last night, when enquiry was made, attending customers in the shop.' The request was refused.[96]

As Hughes and the other local men served out their prison terms, their wives and children had the task of righting upended stalls, buying new produce and resuming the challenge of daily business life.

In the troubled years that followed, the market was placed under regular curfew. Throughout the War of Independence and the Civil War, from their little room above the shop at Little Denmark Street, my grandfather's family watched nightly for Black and Tan patrols. The family, along with many other locals, had been scornful of the Volunteers because of the destruction visited on their livelihoods, but, like many others, when the leaders were executed they warmed to the cause.

Throughout the War of Independence flowersellers and stallholders helped to hide arms and ammunition. A munitions factory was established in the basement of a bicycle shop in Parnell Street, and a public house on Horseman's Row became a secret rendezvous for Michael Collins. He favoured street hawkers and market delivery men as couriers because they were able to move about the city without attracting suspicion. On one occasion, my great-grandfather Con came home, took a bag of tools and disappeared for three weeks. When he returned, he told his wife that he had been knocking holes in the basement of No. 13 Dominick Street, the former home of the Duke of Leinster, for the Volunteers. Such tactics, first seen during Easter Week, became a staple feature of urban guerrilla warfare.

During the 1930s and 1940s long-forgotten arms stashes were sometimes recovered by local children. In post-revolutionary Dublin, the occasional appearance of a rusty Webley revolver in a game of cowboys and Indians was something hardly to be wondered at.

Dear Madam,

In reply to your letter of the 23rd instant I beg to state that the Committee regret that they are unable at this late date to accept claims for compensation in respect of losses sustained in April last. The latest date for notifying claims, as intimated in the newspapers was 12th August, 1916.

Yours faithfully,

Mrs Mary Plunkett,
    16 Moore Street,
        Dublin.

Above: **Letter to Mary Plunkett of No. 16 Moore Street, notifying her that her claim for compensation had been refused.**

(NAI Property Losses [Ireland] Committee 1916, File 6965, 3/083/34)

Right: **Compensation form for No. 16 Moore Street – last headquarters of the rebel leaders in 1916.**

(NAI Property Losses [Ireland] Committee 1916, File 6965, 3/083/34)

6965

Property Losses (Ireland) Committee, 1916.
51 ST. STEPHEN'S GREEN, EAST, DUBLIN.

Claim for Damages caused during the Disturbances on the
24th April, 1916, and following days.

I
We Mary Plunkett   now residing
at   16 Moore   in the City of   Dublin
County
do hereby solemnly and sincerely declare that on or about the 27 day of April
1916, damage was done to the undermentioned Property, namely :— House

    16 Moore St
and such damage was occasioned to the best of my belief by Rifle Fire
And Looting Looting

And I/We further declare that the Property and Articles specified on the other side were so destroyed or damaged; that the Cost Price of same was as shown in each case; that at the time of the destruction or damage they were respectively of the Values specified under the head "Value of Property at time of Destruction or Damage"; and that, in consequence of such destruction or damage, claim is hereby made for the sums specified under the head "Amount Claimed"; that the Claim is made by me
as Owner   ; and that no person is interested in
the said property except MySelf

and that it is not insured by me or any other person, § except as follows, namely :—

                    Company, Policy No.   Amount £
    "   "   "   £
    "   "   "   £

And I/We make this solemn Declaration conscientiously believing the same to be true, and by virtue of the provisions of the Statutory Declarations Act, 1835.

Made and subscribed the 23   day of
                         1916, at 23 St.
                         in the said City,
                         County,
before me, a Justice of the Peace for the said
                         City of Dublin
                         County
Signature
of Claimant Mary Plunkett   John O'Gan JP
Claimants

Note—This Claim is to be furnished in duplicate, and should be accompanied by the Policies of Fire Insurance and the last receipt, in each case, or certified copies of same. When completed it is to be forwarded to the Secretary of the Committee, 51 St. Stephen's Green, East, Dublin.

Cole's Lane. Business slackened there during the Emergency. *(Courtesy of Dublin City Library and Archive)*

The Emergency, 1939-45

The outbreak of the Second World War, known euphemistically in Ireland as 'the Emergency', had a very direct impact on Moore Street and the surrounding market area. Water tanks were placed at various locations such as Horseman's Row in case of fire, and a house at the corner of Denmark Place was once set alight as a training exercise for the Auxiliary Fire Service.[97] In nearby Dominick Street, concrete air-raid shelters appeared almost overnight.

For the most part, however, the effects of the war were felt economically rather than physically. In September 1939 fishmongers were among the first traders to feel the pinch, when Irish trawlers refused to venture out to sea for fear of mines. Wartime censoring ensured that newspaper reports of this were suppressed in favour of a more banal explanation, but, whatever the truth, the price of fish in the city soon began to rise. Large dealers found that they were unable to fulfil long-standing orders with hospitals and other institutions. O'Hanlon's of Moore Street told an *Irish Press* reporter that they had to pay 200 per cent over the pre-war price.[98] Soon, over twenty fish workers from the South City Markets, O'Hanlon's and Dunne's of D'Olier Street were given notice.

Another unforeseen consequence of the shipping disruption was that the city's medical schools could not obtain their usual supply of rats from Britain for dissection. For young Seamus Marken, it was an opportunity to make money:

> They came down to Moore Street and met my Uncle Mick. They provided a cage and about twelve smaller ones. The big cage was for keeping the rats in and the others were to trap them. We put these in the backs of the butchers' shops during the day. The next day we'd go around with a special box and collect any live rats. We brought them down to a cellar, put them into the big one, fed them and watered them. The college gave us 1s 9d per live rat. A pint at that time was about 8d so you'd get nearly three of those for the cost of a rat. Before long, we had more rats than the college would want.[99]

That Christmas it was still possible to buy imported fruits such as bananas and oranges, and some enterprising business butchers ran advertisements in the evening newspapers, reminding readers that they could send a gift of meat to friends or relatives in England.

Bananas were still available in the market during the early part of the war.

(Courtesy of Dublin City Library and Archive)

YOUR FRIENDS IN ENGLAND NEED MEAT

SEND A GIFT, 4 lbs. (2 Beef and 2 Mutton). EXPERTLY PACKED by us.

Country customers save time by letting us send direct. (Our parcels arrive in excellent condition in approximately 2 days). CHOICEST CUTS. 4lbs. 12/6 (including Registered Post and packing). Full Price List on request. Send Cheques and P.O. payable to:

CHARLES McALESTER,

Wholesale and Retail Butcher.
33 MOORE STREET, DUBLIN. TELEPHONE 73273.

Advertisement from the *Sunday Independent*, 17 November 1946.

As the war began to take hold, the government's Department of Supplies, located in Ballsbridge, issued ration books and monitored the controlled prices set for key commodities. This stipulation extended to what went on sale in the market. However, Moore Street's traders struggled to sell at the controlled price, particularly when goods became more expensive to buy. The problem was compounded by a severe frost that in 1940 destroyed large crops of the York cabbage upon which Dubliners had come to rely.

People soon realised that a number of supposedly rationed goods could still be bought under the counter in Moore Street without a coupon. As a result of this kind of black-market trade, thrifty shoppers with a certain ration allowance for sugar or white flour might buy what they needed (albeit above the odds) and keep the coupon to get more of these goods elsewhere. In order to combat this illicit trade, the Department of Supplies employed 'spotters' or mystery shoppers who were sent into the shops to see what they could buy without a coupon book. On 6 October 1942, Donlon Brothers of Moore Street was fined £40 by the district judge for selling 1 pound of white flour to one of these agents for a value above the controlled price.[100] The area also came to the notice of the authorities when heavily regulated items such as soap and candles were found on sale. In February 1945 Bridget Mooney of Henrietta Flats was fined for three offences of selling candles over the controlled price. Mary Kearns of Henrietta House, Bolton Street, was found guilty of selling onions at 8d a pound (the controlled price was 6d).[101]

Although the authorities were aware that goods were being bought and sold on the black market, they were unable to discover the source of the supply. In the decade that followed, Maureen O'Carroll, Irish Labour Party politician from 1954 to 1957, set up the Lower Prices Council to address this problem. She campaigned not just against such black marketeering, but also against high prices and scarcity.

As the war intensified, the traders on Moore Street showed great charity towards hardship cases. One such concerned the 'Little Mother', a sixteen-year-old girl called Chrissie Cronin, whose family had to leave their Buckingham Street home when it was damaged by German bombs in 1941. She was rehoused in nearby Ballybough, along with her three brothers and one sister, but the subsequent death of their mother left them orphaned. In order to keep the family together, young Chrissie took a casual job and cooked, sewed and knitted at home. She also helped sick neighbours with their housework. The case only came to public notice when the authorities tried to send Chrissie's brothers away to a school, but the Children's Court judge was so overwhelmed by the account of how well Chrissie had looked after them that he decided to raise a collection. Her story also tugged at the heart strings of the Moore Street traders, who gave her a 'deluge' of gifts.

Other examples of the traders' generosity are also recorded. On most days an empty cart was sent down from the local orphanage and filled with fruit and vegetables, all free of charge. People who were down on their luck might ask for an onion, carrot or a sprig of parsley to make a pot of soup. One woman recalled how her mother used to barter with Rosie Johnson, Queen of Moore Street, for food: 'She used to take aul things off me mother just to give her something back – there was no set price; they could be clothes me mother had brought down that were too small for us. No matter. Rosie always had someone lined up for them.' Likewise, trader Catherine (Kitty) Campion recalls, 'Anyone that was poor, I pitied them. A good heart never wants.'[102]

That did not mean that a petitioner could not occasionally overdo it. Once, a man got his thrupence-worth of pot herbs and went to the next dealer to ask for a penny onion. 'Go on,' she said, 'and get your penny onion where you got yer feckin' pot herbs!'[103]

During the final years of the war, imported goods such as bananas and oranges began to disappear from the market, to be replaced with home-grown apples and pears. However, the increased cost of labour, transport and packing meant that such substitutes were outside the reach of the average city household. Soon, many bought no fruit at all.

There were also severe meat shortages. In response, the members of Dublin's Master Victuallers' Association set up a number of supply depots across the city. To make matters worse, in June 1945 several hundred butchers, porters and messengers of the Workers' Union went on strike in demand of an extra week's holiday per year with pay. They picketed a large number of butchers' premises. One of the worst flashpoints was Moore Street, which housed two association depots. On 8 July 1945 there was a clash during which a window of the supply depot was smashed and adjacent fruit and vegetable stalls were upset. The Gardaí drew batons and made three arrests.[104]

As beef and pork continued to climb in price, alternatives had to be found. Rabbits, known locally as 'grazers', had been sold in the market for years, but now they became a staple of household diets. Many butchers also manufactured a cheaper alternative to butter. Christy O'Leary (aged sixty-nine) recalls that his father had a rendering yard where beef dripping was made: 'They used to render all the fat and boil it down. Then they put it into buckets and sold it the same way you buy a pound of butter. That was a great cholesterol injection!'[105]

There was no doubt that many traders struggled to survive. In response to the hard times they adopted a thrifty attitude. Seamus Marken recalls:

> If you went into the shop, my grandmother would say, 'Pick up that penny.'
> You could go blind looking for it without seeing it. Do you know what
> she meant? The wooden skewers that they used in the shop – they cost a
> penny each. The little hooks that they used for hanging up the chickens
> were three pence so likewise, she'd say, 'Pick up that thruppence.'[106]

Inevitably, some age-old customs began to change in the market. Families who had passed their stalls down through several generations saw their daily business plummet dramatically as a new economic reality began to take hold. A reporter for *The Irish Times* described the situation thus:

> As I walked down Cole's Lane in the rain yesterday … proprietors sat
> beneath sodden awnings, stoically awaiting the customers who seldom
> come, and dreaming, perhaps, of the pre-war days of Dublin's *bourgeois*
> plenty, when second-hand salesrooms were bursting with goods, and
> prosperous working-class buyers thronged the market.[107]

By 1943 stallholders were so worried about this state of affairs that they began to send their sons and daughters to technical schools or get them apprenticeships in shops. Many of these children returned regularly to help out or to visit their parents. However, if a girl were to return to the market with any airs or graces, she was soon brought back to earth. 'I knew your family well,' the retort would come. 'Didn't youse used to live in a back room in Dominick Street?'

During the war, it was too expensive for the traders to buy tea in the local cafés so they shared communal bagging cans. An ounce of tea cost half a crown. Mary Manley recalled that 'you would often prefer a cup of tea to a bit of dinner, it would be that cold out here'.[108]

On 3 December 1945 oranges reappeared on Moore Street for the first time, a sign that things were on the mend. Most of the large shops were unwilling to sell the fruit at the control price of 7d a pound, however, claiming that this would not leave any profit. To the street traders, this was a golden opportunity. Ellen Palmer bought the first cargo of oranges and wholesaled them out among the traders who were able to claim a virtual monopoly on the first day's sales. The scene on Moore Street was chaotic as passers-by abandoned handcarts, bicycles and prams to join the rush on the stalls. One dealer sold her entire stock of two cases of oranges in twenty-five minutes, despite the fact that each item sold for 3d (or 12d per pound), well over the controlled price.

Concerned about what was going on, a number of the larger fruiterers convened at 28 Upper O'Connell Street and sent a telegram to the secretary of the Department of Industry and Commerce: 'Oranges being sold freely at street corners and in Moore St and Henry St at 3d and 4d each, equivalent to 1/- and ½ a lb. Total disregard shown your price control. Request immediate action.'[109]

As the day wore on, the Gardaí were called in to keep order and the ground was littered with peel. One dealer, stopping to catch her breath, was heard to say, 'I'll need a glass of whiskey after this rush. In a few days, we'll be coaxing you people to buy oranges.'[110]

There was a lapse of about two weeks before the next consignment of 18,000 half cases arrived from Valencia on the Limerick Steamship Company's *Lanahrone*. It was followed by a consignment of Jaffas. By late January 1946 the first oranges suitable for making marmalade had begun to arrive from Seville.

For local butchers, one unexpected bonus of the war was the sudden availability of ebony-handled jungle machetes. These had been used during the Philippine campaign. 'You could buy them for 1s 6d in Dublin,' Eamon Martin recalls, 'the

Cole's Lane.
(Courtesy of Dublin City Library and Archive)

steel in them was fantastic, and they made great butchers' knives once they were cut down to size.'[111]

Once again, the market traders had seen themselves through a difficult period with fortitude and good humour. The Emergency had come to an end.

Auctioneer at work in the fruit and vegetable
market, Halston Street, c.1930

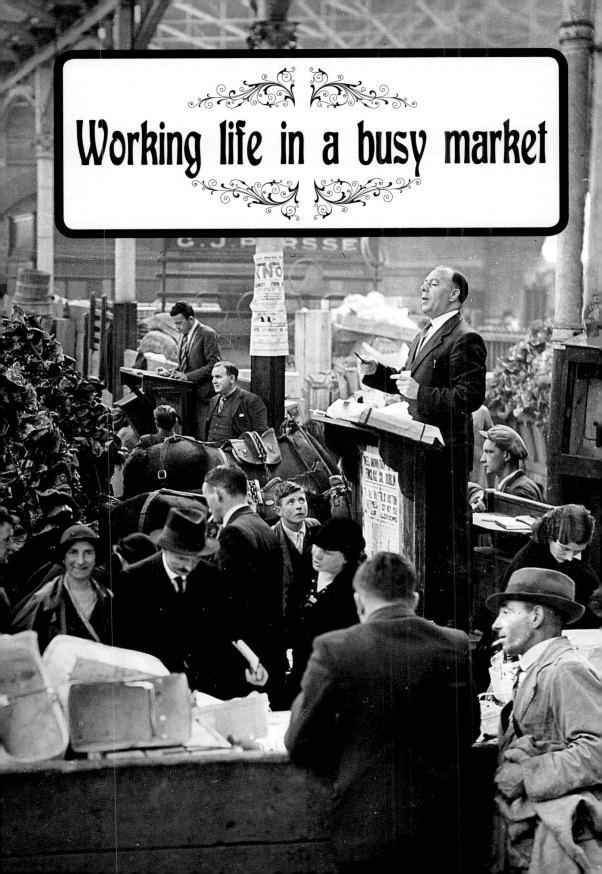

Working life in a busy market

The traders in Moore Street have long held a prime place in Dublin's cultural heart. Many of the scripts that Harry O'Donovan wrote for actor Jimmy O'Dea were based on them. But what few people know is that Biddy Mulligan, 'the Pride of the Coombe', was actually 'born' there too. Historian Éamonn MacThomáis tells the following story about her origins:

> One evening as Jimmy and Harry were walking down Henry Street, Harry said, 'Jimmy, we must get you a particular type of character, something or someone you would be recognised as; Chaplain has his derby hat and walking stick' … Just at that moment a woman came out of a public house in Moore Street shouting at a man behind her – 'Go along outa that, you bowsie.' O'Donovan's eyes twinkled. His mind flashed, his fingers clicked and O'Dea soon got the message. 'That's it,' said Harry, 'a woman of Dublin talking like that woman', and so Biddy was born in the heart of Moore Street.[112]

The ubiquitous Mrs Mulligan had good reason to be such a hard ticket: she had a large family to raise and needed to be ready for whatever life had to throw at her. A typical day on Moore Street usually started at about half past five in the morning. Before going to work, many of the traders stopped to attend Mass in Dominick Street or to say a quick prayer at a shrine to Matt Talbot in Granby Row. They might drop a small coin or two into the offerings box for luck before starting their long day.[113]

Afterwards they paid a visit to the fish market, or the fruit and vegetable market in Green Street – a marvel of Victorian engineering. It was handsomely decorated with clumps of terracotta onions, fruit and vegetables, and built to be north-facing, thus avoiding intense sunlight, with a set of three ventilation laths on either side in a roof crevice running the length of the building. This helped to ensure that produce was kept cool, even during the summer months. Prior to its construction, fruit, vegetables and flowers had been auctioned at local open-air venues such as Anglesea Market, off Capel Street. The new market, situated adjacent to the chicken, fish and clothes (Daisy) market, gave the traders some protection from biting winds and heavy rains. Inside, the clang of the auction bell sounded in vain over the sound

Jane O'Leary pictured at her stall, *c.* 1900.
(Courtesy of the O'Leary family)

of haggling and hard bargaining on the floor. Justin Leonard, whose grandmother was the first woman to have a stand there after it opened in 1892, details the scene:

> The market opened at 7 o'clock, and all the companies there were auctioneers; you had to be a member of the association. The first hour from 7 a.m. to 8 a.m. was for the growers to bring their produce in. The bulk, if not all, of the vegetables came from North County Dublin by horse and cart. Growers didn't come from further afield as it wouldn't have reached the market quick enough.

Street traders depart for Moore
Street with handcarts, *c.* 1940.
(Courtesy of Bill Cullen)

The farmers would pull up with their horses and carts at the top of the market. It was a queue system, so whoever was there first got in early with his produce. Each grower supplied a particular company. When the carts came in, they would pull up outside the stands or 'banks'; these were all raised up about a foot off the ground.

There was no packaging, boxes or bags. Everything on the cart was packed loose. For instance, cabbages were stacked, 144-dozen heads, onto the back in a pyramid. It was an art in itself. Then the doors were opened to let the buyers in and the auctioneers would start bidding off. Whoever

Moore Street – *c.* 1930. (*Courtesy of Terry Fagan*)

gave the biggest price would get the cart of cabbage or whatever the produce was. That set the price.[114]

The first buyers of the day were typically shopkeepers. After them came the Moore Street traders. The by-laws of the market aimed to encourage competition and to oppose a monopoly on trade, but a trader still needed to keep her wits about her. There was no refund for buying bad fruit or vegetables. Dealers from certain streets or areas tended to stick together. For instance, people from Gloucester (Sean MacDermott) Street clubbed in with others from that street. The same went for people from Greek Street or from Summerhill. Working together had its advantages, since traders could pool their money and buy a pallet of produce.

Next, their goods needed to be transported back to Moore Street. Some women

Moore Street, 27 October 1961. *(Courtesy of the National Library of Ireland)*

walked, wheeling iron-wheeled wicker-basket cars through the laneways. For larger consignments, the menfolk, otherwise unemployed, could be found pushing handcarts or helping to load the horses and carts that plied between the market and Moore Street several times a day. Bernie Shea (aged seventy-five) recalls that on arrival, 'The dray would go up in the air, a bolt would be pulled back and all the cabbage would be in the gutter. The dogs and cats would be running all around it but we never died of poisoning.'[115]

The fish traders had a different arrangement. Early in the morning, their trays of herring, whiting and cod were usually delivered to the empty 'stannin' and left there covered by ice.

Now the day was truly under way. For transactions, each trader wore a 'pocket', a large apron tied around the waist with compartmented sections for holding notes

Moore Street *c.* 1960 – note the line of housing (top right) where the Ilac Centre now stands. *(Courtesy of Eamon Martin)*

and loose change. These couldn't be bought in a department store and had to be specially made. The prospect of losing one spelt financial ruin, as one interviewee recalls:

> An aunt of mine was after being up [in the flat] and she took her pocket off. She left it and she couldn't find it but didn't I come across it under the bed. It was after being folded up and all the money was in it. She was in an awful state. 'I'm after losing me pocket,' she says. I told her I had it under me pillow because she left it on the floor when she was going out. 'Well do you know what,' she said, 'there was hundreds of pounds in it.' If those pockets could talk, they'd tell many's the story.[116]

It helped to have a sense of humour when standing out all day on a street stall. Traders rarely allowed a customer to pick their own produce: 'Ah, *musha*, is it

Switzer's ya think yer shoppin' in or the Home and Colonial? Comin' here pickin' and choosin' in yer furs an' yer mud-packed facial. God, the airs an' graces of them!'[117]

Dubliners were familiar with the sing-song voices of the traders along the street: 'Penny the apples and oranges.' But that refrain could change abruptly with the arrival of the poor children who swept into the market at various times to lift fruit, vegetables, clothes or shoes. A cry would go out along the stalls: 'Here comes the robbers.'

Herrings from the same source might be sold in separate boxes as 'Dublin Bay' or 'Howth' herrings, thus appealing to individual preference. 'I wouldn't eat them Howth herrings,' someone might be heard to say. In reality, there wasn't a bit of difference.

Outside on the street, barefoot children could be seen congregating around their mothers, who sat on upturned boxes minding their stalls. From time to time the familiar bang of a captive bolt pistol could be heard from the slaughterhouses nearby. The children, along with their counterparts from Dominick Street or Henrietta Street, nosed around them for pig or sheep bladders, which they inflated by mouth, tied off and used as footballs. At other times they scavenged for mislaid rounds on the bloody floors of the slaughterhouses and took them away to strike against the cobbles. Seamus Marken recalls one childhood game:

> The dealers used to get wooden crates of oranges and they were bound with a rope; they'd take the rope off very carefully and they'd sell it to us for maybe tuppence. There was a warren of little lanes off Moore Street and we knew every one of them … it was a kind of a chasing game; say two guys would chase you and if they caught you they'd tie you up with your own rope and you'd be left there maybe in an aul' doorway, hoping one of your pals would come around and release you.[118]

An astute youngster could earn a penny by grinding mangolds for cattle as they wintered in Foley Street or by helping to keep them out of the side streets as they were driven to slaughter. During the summer, there was little difficulty in helping out on the stalls, but in the winter it was pure hardship. This is captured very poignantly in a poem, 'The Angel' (1946) by J. H. Orwell:

Today I saw an angel, saw her stand
On the frozen pavement with small red splayed toes,
A little, mud-splashed angel, by the lane
That leads to Moore Street market; with one hand
She scratched a tangled halo, and with one
She gripped a ragged one-legged teddy-bear.[119]

Many of the stalls were temporary affairs, built from crates, but some were purpose-built with wheels underneath. By the 1970s a trader had to pay 50 pence a year in order to sell from one on Moore Street, but the passing trade was brisk. Prior to the 1980s the road was not pedestrianised, which brought a lot of carts, jarvey cars and, later, motorised vehicles rumbling past.

During the summer months, it could get very hot and dusty. Some traders wore wide-brimmed hats or cabbage leaves to keep the sun off their heads. Martin 'Willie' Higgins (aged sixty) recalls, 'There were two dealers on either side of me mother. One sold fish and another chickens. The helicopters [flies] would be flying around them; the meat would be hanging up, and, Jaysus, it'd be nearly cooking.'[120]

Bad weather kept the flies away, but it also made for poor business. The rain sent potential customers scurrying indoors, but the traders had no such luxury. They wore rubber boots known locally as 'kossicks', stuffed with newspaper to keep out the cold. On wet days some wore potato sacks, tied front and back. Although the street traders did not drink very much, they might take a glass of hot whiskey in the snug of a local pub to offset the cold.

Rosie Johnson, the first Queen of Moore Street, was in a class of her own in that regard. This indomitable woman, who had given Alexander Scott (better known as Hector Grey) his first start by allowing him to sell razor blades near her stall, was born at No. 12 Moore Street in 1891. She continued to live there until the building was condemned during the 1960s. Rosie began selling violets on the street at a penny a bunch, and in later years used to drink a bottle of stout openly in the street – admittedly pressed into her hand by eager tourists. She is recalled in the song 'Rosie up on Moore Street', written by Pete St John and first recorded by his good friend Sean Dunphy:

Left: Rosie Johnson (1891–1987), Queen of Moore Street. This picture was taken at Owl Studios, 3 Henry Street, *c.* 1930. Note the sprig of Shamrock.

Below: Rosie Johnson as she was known to locals and tourists in later life.

(*Courtesy of Eamon Martin*)

The market behind Moore Street sold more than clothes. Here, a man browses among second-hand household goods, *c.* 1930.
(*Courtesy of Terry Fagan*)

Oh Rosie up in Moore Street, tipplin' 'neath her shawl,
The old ball of malt and the chaser,
Oh Rosie she was neat, ah the queen of all the street,
Cos Rosie was the dealers' darlin'.

Although they have now disappeared, buskers were a regular feature of the street until the 1960s. The instruments of choice were banjos and harmonicas, all of which helped to create a good selling atmosphere.

Trade on the street peaked at noon and again at about three o'clock in the afternoon. During the interlude, a dealer might relieve the monotony with a cup of tea or a glass of stout. One of the four public houses on the street was Leahy's in Sackville Lane (O'Rahilly Parade), which had a side entrance for women. The publican there obliged the dealers by boiling billy cans of water so that they could make tea. Bernie Shea recalls that when Maggie, one of the traders, died, her last wish was to be buried with two large bottles of Guinness – a request that was duly honoured.

Away from the pavement, the street's butcher shops had their own daily routine. Until the mid twentieth century, they had no shop windows and displayed their meat on hooks at the entrance to their premises. Flour-powdered chickens and skinned rabbits were sold off marble-top tables. Fowl were transported to the shops live in wooden crates, but pig's cheeks, ribs and backbones were sold from pickle barrels. Seamus Scully recalls: 'Under the tables lay the sheeps' and cows' heads dripping with blood – and with their stark eyes – which a few days previously had been driven up the street by the shouting drovers, followed by yelling youngsters beating the animals with sticks.'[121]

Inside the shops, there was no queue system. Instead, customers jostled shoulders with each other in an attempt to catch the proprietor's attention. One of the first butchers to advertise on the street was Troy's, who used to ring a bell to attract customers. Later on, technology was employed. Eamon Martin of Martin & Son recalls:

> I had two super Akai, open reel tape recorders, and I would advertise into the street – not very loud, keeping it so low that people would want to get near to the window to hear it. The result of that was that we packed the shop. The next thing, I decided that there must be some way of putting order into this gang of customers. There was a very famous pork shop on Henry Street called Hafner's. It was very busy, and if you were a child, God help you, you were overlooked. It was terrible. I was the first retailer in Dublin to have a queue system. It took three weeks to get it organised, and we did it. I served people from the right, *only*. The rest is history.[122]

The network of adjacent lanes and alleys, although connected with Moore Street, was like another world. Actor Garrett Keogh, whose great-grandmother had a business on one side of Riddall's Row, with his grandmother on the other, recalls:

Our shop was on the corner of Norfolk Market and Riddall's Row. The family had another place opposite that they rented to Willie and Paddy – a father and son who were upholsterers and antique repairers. There were furniture shops there too – you couldn't get into some of the rooms because everything was packed full of items for sale. They would be dragged out in the morning and put on display.

The front walls were made of wooden shutters (that was general in the market). The first shutter or door was on a hinge that opened – maybe about two and a half foot wide. The next one slid out along a little groove. They'd take the shutters out and stack them up against the wall. Then they'd take out little A-frame stanchions, lay the doors on them, cover them (sometimes with sheets) and put their wares on top.[123]

Among the traders who dealt in clothes, shoes and other commodities in the market's interior, one of the best known was John Clarke, after whom the nearby Trader John's public house was named. He used to travel the city on a bicycle collecting second-hand garments and other goods.

Those who dealt in shoes got them at auction rooms on Wellington Quay or Francis Street. They had come from pawnshops all over the country. Auctions were

Trader John's, which closed in 2005, was the last remaining public house on Moore Street.
(Courtesy of Moore Street Lending Library, 2005)

usually held a couple of evenings a week and canvas postbags were used to transport the shoes back to the stalls the following morning.

Some traders were very enterprising, as Garrett Keogh recalls:

> My grandmother Maggie May used to go to Glasgow. She would close up the shop in Riddall's Row on a Tuesday evening and take one of the children (generally my mother) with her. They used to take a taxi down to the North Wall and catch the overnight boat. The route entailed a long trip up the Clyde Canal, which took nearly as long as the rest of the journey, so her friends used to meet her at the mouth and drive her the rest of the way. Once she got the shoes she wanted there, they were all sent down to the ship. She'd do a little bit of shopping then and come back that same night.[124]

Once the shoes arrived back at the market, they were stretched and had their creases removed. Then they were polished and sent to the menders to be half-soled or heeled if necessary. Many Dubliners could not afford to buy such items outright, however, so some locals dispensed shoe dockets – a loan system that allowed people to pay for their footwear in regular instalments.

Brendan Behan's brother Dominic recalled the following visit to Cole's Lane with his mother as a child:

> All along the two sides of the narrow passage behind the shops in Moore Street were stretched rows and rows of little stalls, piled high with everything from silk knickers to dirty white surgical stockings. The ladies in charge of the various portable emporiums were considerate and mannerly until it was obvious to them that Ma was not easily satisfied. 'Are yeh buyin', girl? There's a lovely pair of hair striped pants, worn only on the left side because the man who left them off had only one leg. I could let yeh have them for half-nothin', mam, since I'm nearly sold out … for Jaysus sake, don't mess up the goods if yeh've no intention of buyin'!'[125]

A similar experience is recounted in Michael O'Beirne's *And the Moon at Night*: 'All the second-hand suits here were perfect,' he recalled, but 'the gruesome thing about

Returning to the stores – 'Magzo' Reid and Paddy Wright, *c.* 1960.
(Courtesy of Dublin City Library and Archive)

second-hand gents' clothing was that someone must have died in them, or been hurried off to prison leaving them behind.'[126]

The stall traders or owners of the various shops could be your best friend on days when they were in good form. At other times, when fortunes were low, one might encounter them looking sullenly at their wares.

Flowers had always been sold on Moore Street as well as at Nelson's Pillar. Displayed in wicker baskets, they tended to be native varieties from the Strawberry Beds: primroses, pansies, violets, cowslips, daisies or marguerites. Occasionally these were supplemented by imitation roses and petunias. Maggie Wade, who had been selling at the 'Nile Side' of the Pillar since 1868, recalled in 1941:

> We were there before they put the railing round the Pillar, when it was known as 'the City Sofa' because of all the young gentlemen that used to lounge on the steps criticising the fine ladies in their grand carriages … the young swanks would stop their carriages at the Pillar and buy posies for the ladies. The fine weather men we called them. They'd always greet you with: 'Fine weather ma'am.'[127]

During the 1960s more exotic blooms began to appear: this was made possible by refrigeration.

In the evening time the remaining fruit and vegetables were taken to lock-up facilities off Moore and Sampson's Lanes. Although many traders sold fruit, others specialised in less perishable vegetables, such as parsnips and turnips. Bernie Shea recalls, 'When you'd be going into the stores, you'd sing all the songs you knew because of the rats. I'd a lovely voice. Maria Callas had *nothing* on me. You'd make noise and you'd kick the door but the rats would mind their own business and stay hiding.'[128]

Their day's work done, the traders would repair to one of the area's many pubs such as Dwyer's, Madigan's or Maher's, rubbing shoulders with Radio Éireann people from the GPO as they counted their day's takings over a glass of stout. The busiest days of the week were Fridays and Saturdays, but they could look forward to a day off on Sunday and Monday. Afterwards they had their families to feed, before the busy round of market life began all over again.

Siobhan Hegarty's stand, Moore Street, December 2011.
(Courtesy of Tommy Nolan)

Selling Christmas holly in the market, *c.* 1940.
(Courtesy of Leonard & Sons)

Christmas on Moore Street

December has always meant a seasonal windfall for the Moore Street market, particularly with the arrival of additional customers from the country. During the early 1900s butchers could be found binding their mutton with red ribbon and festooning geese, pheasants and guinea fowl with paper decorations. Later, tinsel was added to shop displays. Several years after that, market activities began to spill over onto the adjacent Henry Street in a fairly colourful way. Some of the permanent fruit and vegetable sellers left their stalls for an entire month and went onto Henry Street.

By the 1950s seventy-four seasonal licences were being given out each year. Various items were sold, from paper Christmas decorations and balloons, to the famous wind-up 'Cheeky Charlie' on his little tricycle. A decade or so earlier, his counterpart had been the wind-up aeroplane, pecking hen or wagging dog. Practically all of these items were purchased from Hector Grey, the famous fancy-goods wholesaler in Liffey Street, or from the Northlight Razorblade Company at the rear of Walden's in Granby Row.

Other items for sale were handmade, as Bernie Shea recalls:

> Even before I made me Communion, I used to cut down the branches [twigs] up in the Phoenix Park for making flowers. Then I'd walk home where I had crêpe paper in sheets. You cut it in sections, put it on your knee and rolled it hard. That would put a curl on it. Then you'd wrap it around the branch and tie it up with wire or an aul string. We used to stand in Henry Street for the month of Christmas and sell the flowers for so much a bunch.[129]

Setting up time was 7 a.m., with the section between Moore Street and the Pillar considered best for selling. From that time onwards, the street would be filled with boxcars, handcarts, prams, and horses and carts. Only one side of the street was

BIG WORDS, BUT TRUE

—— I AM OFFERING ——

Ten Thousand Hams

From all the Best Irish Curers at extraordinary Low Prices

You can have the exact size you want, and just the Cut you want. You can have quick service and civility, and your goods delivered anywhere.

There is no doubt the Christmas Dinner
Is the best for the year of all meals;
If you want it just simply perfection,
Then come buy your ham at John Sheil's.

Specially Reduced Prices For All Groceries and Provisions

Note only Addresses :

JOHN SHEIL

WHOLESALE AND RETAIL PROVISION MERCHANT

6½, 8 and 9 MOORE STREET,
45 and 46 MANOR STREET,

'Phones: 48537, 43538, 23113.

Largest Stock in Dublin to select from

Above: Butcher's advertisment, 14 December 1932.
(Picture courtesy of the Irish Newspaper Archive)

Left: Alexander Scott, better known to Dubliners as 'Hector Grey', *c.* 1970.
As a racetrack turf advisor, he borrowed his trading name from a famous Australian jockey. *(Courtesy of Eamon Martin)*

The staff of Martin's Butcher Shop, No. 55 Moore Street, in 1972. *Front row:* Paddy Carroll, Eamon Martin, Lily O'Carroll; *back row:* —, —, Joe Eglington, Tommy Brennan. *(Courtesy of Eamon Martin)*

Liam (Bill) Cullen, Julie-Ann Jolley, unnamed child, Jinny Foster, unnamed child, *c.* 1950. *(Courtesy of Bill Cullen)*

available for traders each day, with the pitch alternating throughout the week to give shops a brief respite.

For traders and their families, December provided a much-needed source of income – useful when it came to weddings or communions. Fathers were drafted in for security, with entire families pitching in to ensure the success of the venture.

During the 1950s a number of street traders from Thomas Street and the Liberties began to cross the Liffey. They slowly established an annual seasonal presence on Henry Street, but were not allowed to conduct their business sitting down. Neither could they use stationary fixtures such as tables. In an attempt to get around this obstacle, they sold from shoulder-slung baskets, upturned boxes and trays perched on a raised leg.

Bill Cullen recalls that his mother, Mary Darcy, was not prepared to give up her pitch without a fight:

> 'Who might you be?' she asked of a big stout woman, dressed in a tight brown overcoat, not a shawl. 'And what do ya think you're doing here on my mother's pitch that she has a licence for since before you were born?'
>
> The woman was taken aback and glanced at a tough-looking man on the footpath. It was he who replied. 'We're the Barrys from the Liberties and we've a street-trading licence so we're entitled to sell here if we want to,' he said brusquely.[130]

Undoubtedly, Mary Darcy was a robust woman. If Rosie Johnson was the Queen of Moore Street, Mary was 'the Boss'. She kept a poker by her side as a deterrent in times of trouble and was often called upon by traders for help.[131] Some were able to maintain their hold on the street, but those who were a little weaker found themselves displaced by the newcomers. Eventually people began to keep all-night vigils on their pitches, sleeping in doorways along Henry Street to ensure that their spot was not taken.

Today, Christmas continues to be a vibrant part of the market calendar, bringing Henry Street to life and injecting a bit of vitality into the heart of the city.

The Kennerk family of No. 17 Norfolk Market, *c.* 1908. Pictured from left to right are Jack (John Christopher) Kennerk, Margaret Austin (mother), Harriet Kennerk (standing), Lillie Kennerk, Cornelius Kennerk (father) and the author's grandfather, Con Kennerk (junior). Con is wearing a dress-like frock meant to 'disguise' him as a girl – the consequence of a superstition that young boys could be spirited away by fairies. *(Author's collection)*

Traditions and superstitions

Market people had their own traditions. Unsurprisingly, many concerned themes of birth and death. It was considered lucky, for instance, for an infant child to be born in the 'caul' (the membrane around the amniotic fluid). These good omens of childbirth were often kept, and it was not unknown for them to be offered for sale – particularly to sailors as talismans to keep them from drowning. More unlucky were the fairies, harbingers of mischief, who sought out infant boys and swapped them for changelings. In order to prevent this fate, local people often dressed their boys in a flannel dress or frock – a practice that persisted into the twentieth century.

In 1836 the *Protestant Penny Magazine* reported that a coffin, said to contain the body of a saint, had been 'dug up in Cole's Lane' and taken to Gardiner Street Church for veneration. 'Part of the crowd were engaged in devoutly kissing the sides of the coffin,' claimed the account, while others were 'taking the droppings of the lights' or 'detaching pieces from the candles and carefully folding up the scrapings in their handkerchiefs as a grand preservative against all evil.'[132]

Most of those who died in the market area were taken to nearby Glasnevin Cemetery for burial, but the arrival of two coffins at once was believed to be bad luck. The soul of the last corpse to be interred was forever doomed to draw water with a leaky bucket to soothe those in Purgatory. Naturally, neither party wanted such a fate to befall their deceased family member and on one occasion this led to a fight. One Sunday, in July 1835, the members of two separate cortèges made a rush at the cemetery gates. The defeated party was a group of butchers from Cole's Lane. Determined to get their revenge, they returned the following week to meet their opponents, who were attending another funeral. The *Dublin Warder* reported that:

> As soon as it did appear, it was immediately attacked, the coffin and corpse demolished in an instant – two men named Williams and Mulcahy, from the egg-market, were killed, and eight sorely beaten. The speedy arrival of the police prevented further mischief. On Tuesday the coal porters came there to assist their friends, the butchers; but, not meeting any of their opponents, they dispersed at ten o'clock.[133]

THE MOLLY MALONE
STREET TRADERS BARROW
manufactured
J.M. O'TOOLE & SONS LTD. 1 LR. DORSET ST.

Right: **Taking part in the competition for the best-kept stall, 1959.** ***(Courtesy of the National Library of Ireland)***

Market people were also full of old cures and home remedies. They often waded in the animal manure that collected around the slaughterhouses, for instance, believing it to be a cure for chilblains and other such complaints. Seamus Marken recalls:

> For a cut, they used to go into a basement and wrap a spider's web around it. For burns and scalds, they went to Mrs Flood in Cole's Lane, who sold an ointment she made out of pig's lard. She'd give it to you in a big ceramic thrupenny jam jar, but you had to give it back to her afterwards. People preferred those kinds of home remedies instead of the hospital; you'd only get a tetanus shot up there.[134]

One commonly seen sight in the little alleyways was the fortune teller, who pushed a cart with a barrel organ. A cage on the organ held two lovebirds and a box full of tiny envelopes. He used the organ to strike up a tune and attract some business. When the music stopped, he would be surrounded by a crowd. Once a client handed over his or her penny, he would take one of the lovebirds out of its cage and coax it to remove an envelope from the box. The message inside contained the fortune.

In an era prior to television, stories about ghosts and banshees were commonplace. With eyes wide as saucers, children listened to black-shawled old women tell tall tales. By day, these same women could be seen honing their craft as they shared pipe tobacco with their neighbours in the grounds of King's Inns, Henrietta Street.

Other Moore Street traditions are more recent. During the mid 1950s Dublin Corporation inaugurated an annual award-giving ceremony for the best-kept stall. In the 1980s, after some years of apathy, this was replaced by the 'Molly Malone competition' – the concept of Assistant City Manager Davy Byrne, who came up with it while passing the market on a windy day. As he stood amid scattering papers and cartons, he decided that he would need help from local traders to deal with the problem. Each winner would be awarded a cash prize, as well as an engraved tankard, for presentation, cleanliness and friendliness.

Another grand tradition in Moore Street is that of the 'Queen', an honorary title given to the oldest trader. It is generally acknowledged that Rosie Johnson was the first of these. May Gorman is the current title holder, but, with the future of the market hanging in the balance, it remains to be seen whether she will be the last.

Mrs Talbot, one of the Moore Street traders.
(Courtesy of the National Library of Ireland)

Participants in the Molly Malone competition, 1984.

Front left to right: Jenny Beggs, Dinah Mulready, Annie Condon, Michael O'Halloran (Lord Mayor), Norah Gallagher, 'Magzo' Reid, Frank Feely (Dublin City Manager), Bernie McCready, Mary Sutton, Mary Graham, —, —.

2nd row: Annie Shannon, May Mooney, Annie Shiels, Maura Keogh, Annie Keogh, Annie Johnston, Mary Lynch (Gaffney), Chrissie Ross (Snr).

3rd row: Annie Carthy, May Fox, Margaret Connolly, Tony Gregory (TD), 'Magzo' O'Brien, —, Kay Dillon, Annie Johnson, —, May O'Brien.

4th row: Lillie Carthy, Bridie Keogh, Maggie Armstrong, Rosie Farrell, Maureen Talbot, Lizzie Byrne.

Back row: Lucy Kennedy, May Manley, —, Sheila Picket, Margaret Cunningham, Peggy Reilly, Joan Haddock (rest unknown).

(Courtesy of Paul Shannon)

Cole's Lane *c.* 1900. John Cash built twenty-four new shops here in 1800 – one of the few developments in the area. *(Reproduced by permission of the Royal Society of Antiquaries of Ireland)*

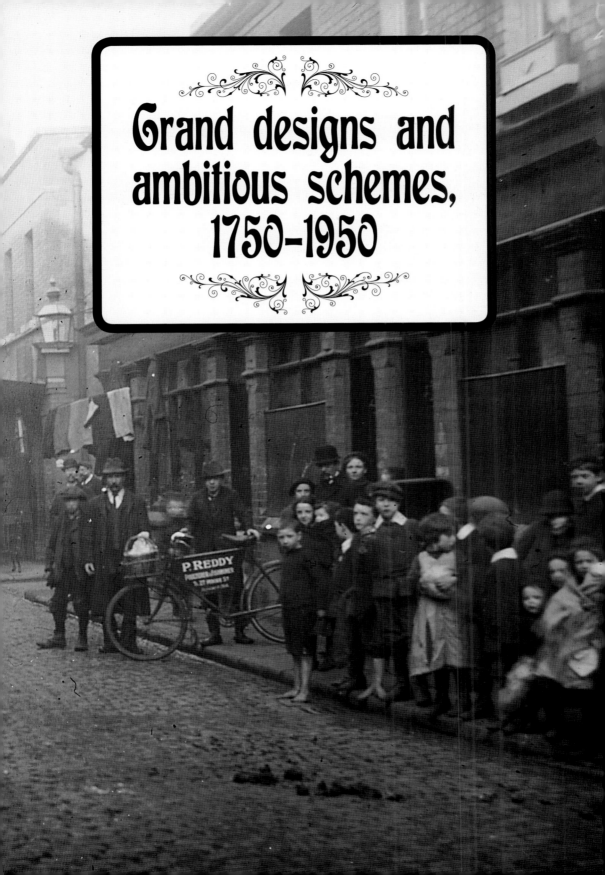

Grand designs and ambitious schemes, 1750-1950

From the late eighteenth century onwards, Moore Street market grew in an unplanned, uncoordinated fashion. As the area became less residential, the long garden plots behind Moore Street and Cole's Lane were built upon for commercial purposes. Alongside such laissez-faire development, efforts were made by the city corporation to make improvements.

During the early 1800s Norfolk and Anglesea markets were constructed to replace the older and less sanitary Walsh's Market. For the most part, however, the following 150 years saw very little real change, despite some very grand proposals. One of the first of these was unveiled at the London Exhibition of 1853 by architect John S. Sloane. He planned to increase the width of the four streets bounding the market area (Great Britain, Henry, Moore and Little Denmark Streets) and to construct new houses and shops. Facing onto Little Denmark Street, communal lodging houses were to be built, each capable of accommodating sixty families. Each dwelling would have a sitting room, two bedrooms, a kitchen, scullery and water closet. By far the most impressive part of the plan was a central, glass-roofed market building, built of iron and with a gallery capable of housing 100 traders (nearly double the number then in business). A great cast-iron column in the centre would store rainwater which could then be used to flush out the floor under the stalls. The whole apparatus was calculated to operate by clockwork at predesignated times.

Sloane also proposed that a number of abattoirs be placed strategically on either side of the building – together these would be larger than all of the northside slaughterhouses combined.[135] Although Sloane's designs attracted a great deal of positive attention, they came to nothing.

The matter of a new market complex did not come to public attention again until 1860.[136] By then, many of the area's buildings were already derelict. Jubilantly, *The Dublin Builder* of 1 December reported a new initiative that would 'rescue this metropolis from the palpable disgrace it has hitherto been labouring under'. A special Act of Parliament would provide for the formation of a company whose task it would be to establish two new markets in the city – one on a site adjoining Cole's Lane and the other on the southside, in the vicinity of Dublin Castle.[137]

When the Bill came under consideration by the House of Commons in 1861, Dublin Corporation, which possessed considerable powers for improving the markets of the city, held a meeting to discuss how it might best be implemented. The new legislation would prevent any selling on streets in parts of the parish outside the designated area. However, some aldermen pointed out that this would give rise to a ludicrous situation whereby a fish seller might sell legitimately on the St Thomas' side of Great Britain Street but be liable to a fine of 40s if she strayed into the area of St Mary's Parish on the other side. Ultimately, the plan was shelved until the area's pavements and sewers had been brought up to an acceptable standard.

During the parliamentary session of 1881–2, the rather lengthily titled Moore Street Market and North Dublin City Improvement Bill was brought before the Commons. Under this legislation, a company was to be formed to raise capital to establish and regulate a new public market on or near the site of the existing one. It would be empowered to acquire property by compulsory purchase, to erect weighing machines and to regulate slaughterhouses. At the same time, plans were drawn up by the city engineer to raze much of the market area with the exception of those premises that faced Great Britain, Moore and Henry Streets. A covered market was to be erected in its place. A similar scheme was already under way off South Great George's Street.

Although the legislation was passed, no action was taken. By 1886 the members of the company, whose mandate was due to expire, had reached a stalemate in negotiations with Dublin Corporation, which believed that it had the sole right to govern the Moore Street market area. Many of its aldermen owned properties there with significant leasehold interests. On 19 January a special meeting was held in City Hall at which the Paving and Lighting Committee was authorised to raise a petition against the North Dublin City Improvement Bill. Its chief object was to form a new market, closing up Anglesea Market, Moore Street Market, Moore Place and Market Street, and widening a number of thoroughfares. A new arcade forty feet wide from Moore Street to Sackville Street was to be formed. While the aldermen generally welcomed any plans to improve sanitation in the area, they deemed the concept of an arcade to be completely useless.[138]

The following year, the corporation tried to act once again. The borough surveyor had reported that fish and vegetables were sold practically on the streets, with a considerable amount of waste produced. The corporation estimated that if these

By the 1930s, many of the older houses in the centre of the market area had disappeared. It was later dubbed 'Tin Town' by locals.
(Dixon slide collection, July 1937, courtesy of Dublin City Library and Archive)

traders were to be charged a fee, the combined tolls and rental, together with the fee for weighing, would provide ample security for a sinking fund to pay off the principal and interest on a £65,000 government loan for a new market house.

Matters reached an impasse. During the early part of 1888, an enquiry was held at City Hall. It was chaired by the local government board inspector, Timothy Healy

MP, who appeared on behalf of the corporation. A number of local traders opposed the scheme. Healy recalled the words of the divisional police magistrate when he said that the area was nothing more than 'a gigantic nuisance and a scandal'.[139] What the traders objected to was not so much the erection of the new market, but the removal of their stalls by the corporation without compensation.

Remarkably, no further schemes for development of the area were proposed until the eve of the First World War. The passage into law of the Dublin Reconstruction (Emergency Provisions) Act on 22 December 1916 empowered the corporation to make compulsory purchase orders and to widen streets. This kept redevelopment of the market on the agenda and some improvements were made, particularly at the Henry Street end of Moore Street and Cole's Lane, where the thoroughfare was significantly widened and rebuilt after the Rising.

In 1932 the Denmark Street and Moore Street Area Compulsory Purchase Order was announced in many of the city's newspapers. In 1935 the corporation housing committee surveyed the area, followed by a visit from the lord mayor and city manager. It was proposed that the Slum Clearance Order be invoked in order to level all the lanes between Moore Street and Little Denmark Street and to erect two large blocks of flats with two new streets in their stead. Compulsory land purchase got under way, until one owner resisted on the grounds that the order had been made under the 1931 Housing Act, even though the land was intended for flats. (The Housing Act at this time did not cover flats.) His case was held up in court, and although the corporation proceeded to buy up property afterwards, it could only do so with the consent of the owners.[140]

In 1940 a compulsory purchase order was once again sought, but new objections were raised. Speaking at an enquiry, the city manager said that, according to the House Committee, the area was one of the worst that the corporation had to deal with in terms of congestion and sanitation. Alderman T. Kelly concurred, adding that Little Denmark Street was 'nothing but a group of ruins'.[141]

This time, however, it was Hendron Brothers, a large machinery merchants, that caused the plans to be put on hold. The company, which employed seventy people, had already made plans to build a new factory in the area, and they hired their own solicitor to represent them. 'It was of the utmost importance,' Francis P. Hendron said, 'that his firm should have large and central showrooms within five or ten minutes' walk of Nelson Pillar.'[142] In his 1942 judgment on the case, Justice George Gavan Duffy once again noted that part of the area was 'a dreadful blot on the city', and he welcomed the corporation's determination to make 'sweeping reforms in a shocking district'.[143]

Nevertheless, Hendron Brothers was granted permission to construct its new premises. It appeared on the Goad insurance map of 1957. By then the area between Rotunda Market and Denmark Place had become nothing more than a large car park with a metal store at its southern end. Denmark Place had completely disappeared, swallowed up by the Hendron development. In the absence of anti-speculation laws, there was no onus on business owners to renovate or redevelop the properties they owned in the area of the market, and, as a result, whole buildings were allowed to decay, fall down and become empty waste ground.

In the meantime, the clothes and shoe traders who lived in the interior of the market area continued to conduct business from premises that had become little more than temporary lock-ups and corrugated sheds with tent-like awnings. Dubbed 'tin-town' by locals, the area was a fascinating, albeit dangerous, place for a child. 'By my time, the shops on Riddall's Row had become lock-ups,' Garrett Keogh recalls. 'They were still two-storey, but the upstairs were fairly derelict and the stairs were falling apart. I'd play in them but be told to come down. Then, some time around the fifties, the corporation condemned them and took the top stories off.'[144] With each year that passed, it seemed as though there was less and less of the original market left to save.

End of an era, 1956–81

Margaret 'May' McDonnell at her shoe shop on Riddall's Row, *c.* 1955. Like many other premises in the area, it had been two-storeyed until the top section was removed by Dublin Corporation. The building seen to the right on the corner of Norfolk Market was an ESB substation.

(Courtesy of Dublin City Library and Archive)

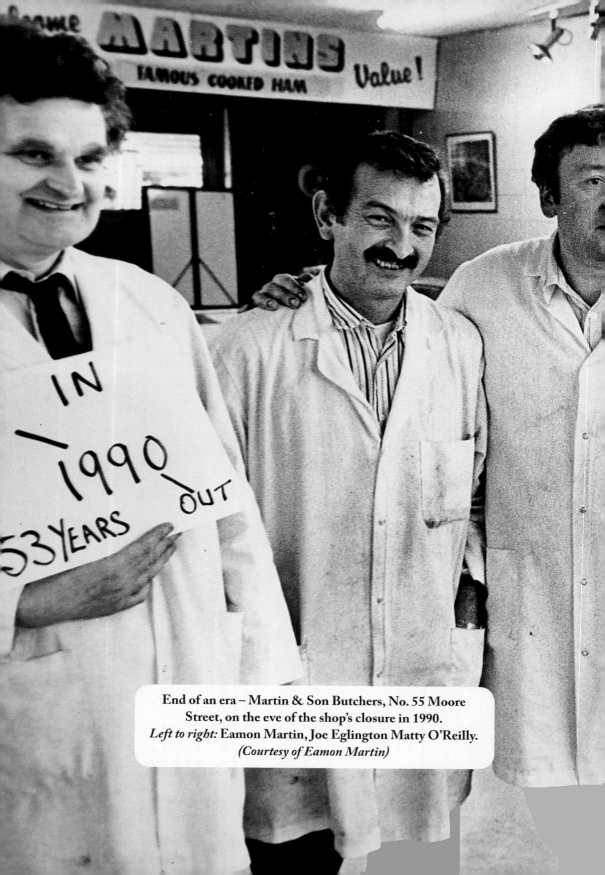

MARTINS

FAMOUS COOKED HAM   Value!

IN 1990 OUT
53 YEARS

End of an era – Martin & Son Butchers, No. 55 Moore Street, on the eve of the shop's closure in 1990. *Left to right:* Eamon Martin, Joe Eglington Matty O'Reilly. *(Courtesy of Eamon Martin)*

In early 1956, when the Moore Street market traders, including long-established families such as the Kennys, Dowdalls, Doyles, Gores and Floods, heard about a new redevelopment plan aimed at relocating the residential community, they hired a solicitor and sent a letter of protest to Dublin Corporation. They were not looking for compensation. Instead, they wanted a small, compact market area, with or without accommodation. A reporter for *The Irish Times* visited the area to gauge local opinions: 'An old woman polishing shoes at a stall looked up at me when I spoke to her. "They'll have to carry me out of here," she said grimly. "I'll lie on the flags and die on them. They'll have to carry me out."'[145]

The corporation filed its plan for the scheme in 1957, but the minister for local government voiced his concerns. He was unhappy with the law under which the plan was governed. In particular, he felt that it did not fully address how slum sites should be acquired for uses other than housing.

In 1960 the government requested the collaboration of a UN expert and, under its programme of technical assistance, an American town planner named Professor Charles Abrams was commissioned to draft a report. His brief was to examine the feasibility of clearing a number of areas in a cost-effective way, one of which included the entire block west of Moore Street. Abrams spent a month in Dublin. During that time he interviewed builders, businessmen, real-estate investors and government officials. He also spoke to the people who actually lived in the area. His report, stark in its reality, brought a new sense of perspective to the issue. For the first time it portrayed the area as seen through the eyes of an outsider:

There are a number of empty lots as one crosses Riddall's Row, while McCann's Lane has a number of old, small, one-storey buildings and a few decrepit two- and three-storey buildings. Contributing to the general drabness are some old slaughterhouses and superannuated storage warehouses fronting on walks which act as the repositories of garbage cans. An empty lot is used for parking, there is a street market on Moore Street while Cole's Lane, a narrow alley, is composed of old one- and two-storey buildings, set among a few vacant lots and shacks.[146]

From an architectural standpoint, there could be little dispute about Abrams' assessment. Many of the old houses and shops in the interior of the market were very dilapidated. Some, such as those in Cole's Lane, had been pressed into use as storage places for stalls or produce.[147] On other streets, steel girders propped up semi-derelict properties. One of the professor's main recommendations was that it would be a waste of public monies to reserve land there for working-class housing.

With the foundations for the new Roche's Stores complex already under way, Dublin Corporation was eager to outline a more extensive commercial development plan for the area. After the passing of the 1963 Planning and Development Act, it redoubled its efforts to acquire a sizeable part of the market by compulsory purchase. This process began in earnest in 1967. The corporation was now empowered to make or carry out arrangements with any person or body for the development of land, similar in some respects to the City Improvement Bill of the 1880s. According to Frank McDonald, there was a 'headlong rush by speculators, auctioneers and other professional wide boys to acquire property in the area ahead of the Corporation [who] turned a blind eye to the methods being used which ranged from straight buy to blackmail and midnight demolition'.[148]

The corporation engaged the services of Dr Nathaniel Lichfield, a planner and economist. His brief was to work with the planning department on an overall scheme for north central Dublin. It encompassed a pilot area of 70 acres, extending to Capel Street on the west and the north quays on the south. He suggested that major shopping expansion should take place in the north of the city in line with consumer patterns.

A number of alternatives of note were considered. The first comprised a redevelopment by the market traders or by a consortium of them. The second was for the corporation to act alone on the scheme. A third option was for redevelopment of the site on a leasehold basis.

Ultimately, it was a fourth option that proved to be the most attractive: a partnership between Dublin Corporation and a major development company.[149] The corporation had come to the conclusion that the area could only be kept alive as a shopping centre. In 1967 it signed a contract with the Irish Property Corporation, a joint venture by British brewer Watney-Mann, Roches Stores and

On the brink of change. Note the construction site hoarding in the top right of the image. Moore Street, *c.* 1979. *(Courtesy of the O'Leary family)*

Star (GB Holdings). A six-acre site was identified. It was bounded by Moore Street, Sampson's Lane, Little Denmark Street (and Nos 33–38 Mary Street), Chapel Lane and Parnell Street. The corporation owned 1.6 acres, with the Irish Property Corporation holding onto a further 2.46 acres. Two acres were to be acquired by compulsory purchase order. The plan, dubbed the 'Heart Transplant', proposed to remove or extinguish the right of way to the little streets within this grid at a cost of £4 million. The area would then be bulldozed and redeveloped. At that point, plans for the new complex were still quite hazy, but some kind of split-level car park was envisaged with a possible subway under Parnell Street.

In response, the area's residents met with representatives from the corporation and formed their own association, which they called the Central Dublin Development Association (CDDA). They hired a barrister, Niall McCarthy, to represent them. What they had in mind was something like the Iveagh Markets, for which they would be prepared to pay a modest rent increase. Some traders, particularly those with furniture shops, realised that they could not be accommodated in a shopping complex since the amount of space they needed was quite large (1,000 square feet and upwards). The cost of rent for such a space would be prohibitive.

Sixty-nine objections were lodged. As a result, under the laws governing compulsory purchase, a local public enquiry chaired by a government inspector needed to be held. When the enquiry opened in the autumn of 1968, James Culleton of the City Architect's office gave evidence. His report detailed the general condition of the area and he produced a map with photographs. Dr Crowe, chief medical officer for Dublin Corporation, was called upon to report on whether the existing houses were suitable for human habitation. His response was largely negative, but he pointed out that it would be possible to carry out repairs. In total, 164 houses, shops, factories, public houses, restaurants and other buildings were to be affected by the compulsory acquisition orders.

In making his report, Culleton found that the butchers' shops on the west side of Moore Street (where the Ilac Centre now stands) were structurally sound. He did not recommend that they be demolished.[150] In general, he praised the traders who had to work under difficult conditions: 'The stalls were so ramshackle … that you could only try to stop leaks and keep flies and rodents away. The traders were working under the hardest of conditions and in my opinion they are deserving of a better fate.'[151]

On 3 October Oscar Garry, a Fellow of the Royal Institute of British Architects, gave evidence. He was one of two architects hired to give their advice on the scheme. Acting on behalf of the CDDA, Mr McCarthy asked some pointed questions of Garry, in particular whether it was possible to build the proposed shopping centre without interfering with Denmark House, a large, early twentieth-century commercial building on Little Denmark Street. When Garry replied that it wasn't an architecturally pleasing building, the barrister quipped, 'Don't you know that it was mentioned in *Ulysses* as a Dublin landmark?'[152]

One corporation inspector remarked that the area badly needed a covered market or some central area for the gutting of fish and dressing of fowl, adding that such matters did not come under the corporation's remit. A health inspector said that he did not believe the courts would allow the corporation to revoke long-standing street trading licences and that the stallholders had a claim on Moore Street.

On 10 October 1968 a number of traders from Riddall's Row gave evidence. They had hired their own barrister independently of the CDDA. Mrs Margaret Keogh told the enquiry that she had been in Riddall's Row for thirty years and that her family had been there for eighty. She explained that her business would not allow payment of a high rent if moved elsewhere and that any compensation would have to be substantial. Another trader, Josephine Farrell from 11 Moore Street Market, explained that:

> We cater for ordinary working-class people, for the women with young children, for the woman who has to keep five or six children on a working man's wages. We can give them shoes at nominal prices. If our rents went up we would have to increase that price so these people could not afford to pay them.[153]

That Christmas there was a huge amount of uncertainty about the new development. Some traders worried that closure of the streets might be imminent and deliberated about whether or not to buy their usual seasonal stock of toys and other fancy goods. The city manager was inundated with calls seeking reassurance. Some traders went so far as to withhold payment of rates until they could get a personal guarantee. Rosie Johnson (then aged seventy-six), told the *Sunday Independent*, 'This is the most famous street in the world. I remember when they ripped up its cobblestones with a buzzer [pneumatic drill]. We want to stay.'[154]

In December 1969 the compulsory purchase order was confirmed by the minister for local government, and almost immediately negotiations began between the development company and the corporation as to how the contract should be implemented. These talks broke down in 1971, as a result of which the corporation engaged the support of a firm of consultants. Messrs Copeland, Novak & Israel, working in cooperation with economic consultant Larry Smith, were commissioned to produce a study scheme and to open the project to tender.

The plan consisted of 100,000 square feet of retail shopping, along with a further

Parnell Street *c*. 1986.
(Courtesy of Dublin City Library and Archive)

300,000 square feet of office space, constructed in two fourteen-storey blocks. A multi-storey car park would be built to accommodate 1,000 cars. Included was a 240-bedroom hotel, 50,000 square feet of leisure space with two cinemas, a theatre, bars and restaurants. All tenders had to be submitted to the local authority evaluation team by 25 May 1973. Eleven were received.

That October, RTÉ aired its *Seven Days* programme. It made a comparison between Moore Street market and its counterpart in Liverpool. There, a strong traders' association had been invaluable in dealing with developers. The newspapers took a bleak view: Dublin did not have a strong track record when it came to such associations, particularly in the long term. On 21 October the *Sunday Independent* interviewed Bennie Callan, the 'Lord Mayor of Moore Street', who told a reporter: 'It'll be the finish of Moore Street. Once they move the stalls out of here, they'll never get them back anywhere else.'

On 30 May 1974 the assistant city manager reported to the city commissioners that, subject to their resolution, government planning and development agency Coisde Pleanála agus Forbairte had approved the granting of a lease on the development site to Irish Life Assurance. Its project architect was David Keane & Partners. The project was to incorporate a theatre, cinema, hotel, two department stores and a covered-over pedestrian mall, constructed in three stages. The property, which extended to 400,000 square feet, was bought in trust by Rathkeale solicitor Michael Noonan.

However, within a few months the plan was scaled back considerably, with the hotel and entertainment complex removed from the brief completely. According to Frank McDonald, this left the corporation's ambitious plan for the area 'in tatters'.[155] It was intended that the shoe and clothing stallholders from Riddall's Row would take up shops in the new centre with rent paid to Irish Life. The move was clearly a concessionary one, since many of the traders had given sworn evidence at the 1968 Inquiry, pointing out that they operated a lucrative business that worked best if they all held together.

On the other hand, rent was not cheap. Irish Life was bound to pay the corporation a capital premium in excess of £1 million and an annual ground rent, subject to review. Instead of a fixed fee, they would pay a percentage of the gross annual sales, with a fixed minimal amount added – a system that was already in place for some high-earning businesses on Henry Street.

Meanwhile, what was left of the market area continued to experience a fall-off in trade. This may have been partly due to the loyalist bombing of Dublin in 1972, in which one of the devices was detonated on Parnell Street, a bus strike that encouraged people to stay out of the city centre and the closure of Moore Street to vehicular traffic – a move that many of the traders had resisted on the basis that it would be bad for business.

The new shopping complex was to be called the Ilac Centre. In order to build it, a large number of old premises on the west side of Moore Street would need to be demolished. These included twelve butchers' shops. The corporation agreed to accommodate some of the traders in prefabricated buildings on Parnell Street, just beyond Horseman's Row, but the traders worried that they would no longer benefit from passing footfall and that the temporary buildings would be burned by vandals. They wanted more permanent structures: three walls of concrete with a secure locked shutter.

The traders had sought an assurance that the development of the shopping centre would proceed in a way that would leave the west side of the street intact until the end, but, rather controversially, demolition of the buildings began a few weeks before any application for planning permission had been made. Garrett Keogh recalls:

> It was a terrible time; these were really good businesswomen, but on a small scale. They were now dealing with big business corporations and legal departments. In the end, they were bought out by compulsory purchase order. My mother took a case to the Court of Arbitration. The developers wanted to buy her out lock, stock and barrel, and have her gone. But she won the right to carry on her trade, and part of the settlement was that she had to be provided with another shop in the development at reasonable rent. She got *buttons* in compensation for city-centre land that she owned, and she was moved around the corner into a prefab. But she was extremely lucky because she discovered Doc Martens – there was a huge market for them.[156]

The Ilac Centre finally opened in 1981. As a gesture, the upper walls of the central rotunda near the public library were decorated with brightly coloured mosaics that depicted life in the old market. These included a bawdy vegetable seller and a man holding up rabbits for sale. Captions recalled the names of some of the streets such

as Norfolk Market and Horseman's Row. In recent years, these mosaics, the only link between the centre and the market it replaced, disappeared for good. Today, little remains to remind the curious visitor of the area that once stood where the Ilac Centre is today.

Furniture shops like this one at No. 27 Little Denmark Street could not be easily accommodated by the new shopping centre development.
(Courtesy of the Irish Architectural Archive)

Angela Wright at her stall, December 2011.
(Courtesy of Tommy Nolan)

Above:
Many local people patronise the hair salons on the street.

Far left:
Comfort Ibitoye, Rachael Ibitoye and Emiola Robert.

Left:
Comfort Ibitoye, proprietor of *Comfort's Salon*, December 2011.
(Courtesy of Tommy Nolan)

In times past, Moore Street traders worked best when operating in tandem with other businesses. The family who came into the market to buy vegetables or meat might also buy a pair of shoes or some good second-hand clothes from Cole's Lane. Working in unison, stallholders benefited from each other.

This kind of business model is now being rediscovered at farmers' markets all across the country, but it was also once crucial to Moore Street's success. The opening of the new shopping complex broke this trading link, sundering fruit, fish and vegetable sellers from shoe sellers and second-hand-clothes dealers who could not afford to move into the expensive new units. For some years, they continued to sell near its Parnell Street entrance, but, inevitably, they disappeared from the scene.

Of course, that was just one factor in the decline of Moore Street market. An influx of cheap foreign clothing and shoes, made possible by Ireland's entry into the European Economic Community, decimated the local rag trade, and it is doubtful that the furniture sellers of Little Denmark Street could have competed with the flat-pack era. Even the fruit and vegetable traders have been overtaken by supermarkets.

That said, Moore Street still continues to attract its stalwart patrons, many of whom are now non-national. The traders have had to adjust as a result and the street now sports a mix of Irish and ethnic shops. One of the first of these opened in 2001 under the proprietorship of Mrs Yu, who recognised that the market was attracting the custom of Chinese students in Dublin.[157] Other shops cater for the needs of Muslims in the city. Salim Ullah Khan, who runs *The Spice of Life*, says:

> Our halal food is in demand and even Irish people are buying it. They find that it is better than what you might buy from a regular butcher. We have a way of draining the blood and tenderising the meat. A lot of people say it tastes much better and cooks quicker too. We sell about 2,000 products, including vegetables that don't grow in an Irish climate.[158]

In October 2009 such changing times were reflected in a five-minute short called *Moore Street Masala*. Produced by Fish Films, it tells the story of a shop clerk called Baba and his infatuation for a local estate-agent girl. Over 300 dancers were

Dance sequence from *Moore Street Masala* –
Ireland's first Bollywood movie. Pictured are
Deva Naidu and Anna Wilson in the lead roles.
(Courtesy of Mark Duffy)

recruited for the final dance number, a Bollywood-style routine that brought a lot of colour into the street. Director David O'Sullivan described the film as a celebration of the Bollywood genre rather than a parody. Equally, *Moore Street Masala* can be seen as a positive affirmation of the changes that have taken place in the market in recent years.[159]

F. X. Buckley's, a long-established butcher shop, has reintroduced pig heads and cow tongues. 'We're doing fish that we've never done before,' says fishmonger Margaret Buckley. 'We used to throw back monkfish, now it's one of the dearest; and then we're doing squid, we're doing sea bass, sea bream, John Dory, fish heads – they make soup out of them. All the foreign nationals know what the fish is and they ask for it.'[160]

However, despite the positive aspects of such changes, there is a danger that what makes Moore Street unique – its long-standing families of butchers, fruit and vegetable traders, flowersellers and fishmongers – will be lost. Keith Duffy, who used to train in a gym called *Unique Physique* on the street, recalls:

On a Friday, we used to buy our fish supper off them – proper tuna steaks, monkfish or a nice piece of salmon. When you're trying to shed body fat to reveal the muscle, you need to eat a high-protein, low-carb diet which is extremely important. Some of the fishmongers on the street would fillet it so you wouldn't have to do that at home. You'd never meet characters like them in the world. It was a great part of Dublin. They'd have a little bit of affection and love for you because you were one of their own.[161]

Sign of the times – a notice in Mandarin and English points towards the Moore Street Lending Library, 2005.
(Courtesy of Moore Street Lending Library)

At the time of writing, all of these businesses – old and new – exist in the shadow of a proposed shopping-centre development. In March 2010 An Bord Pleanála approved plans submitted by Chartered Land, a company owned by shopping-centre developer Joe O'Reilly, for the extension of a new shopping complex from the old Carlton cinema site on O'Connell Street into Moore Street. As part of the scheme, Moore Lane would be extended to join Henry Street to the south. Nos 14 to 17 Moore Street would be preserved as part of a commemorative centre on the GPO 'Garrison Trail', with the façades of Nos 9 and 10 which front onto Moore Street and Henry Place also left in situ. However, that still leaves the remainder of the terrace in the path of the wrecking ball.

James Connolly Heron, great-grandson of James Connolly, takes presidential candidate, afterwards president, Michael D. Higgins on a tour of the Moore Street battlefield site, 10 October 2011.
(Courtesy of Barry Lyons Photography)

Opponents of the scheme, led by members of the Save Moore Street Campaign, who are descendants of the 1916 Proclamation signatories, object on the basis that it would involve major alterations to the old terrace, completely dwarfing it. A report carried out by archaeologist Franc Myles and Shaffrey Architectural Associates, commissioned by Dublin City Council in 2005, identified three main components of the terrace associated with the Rising: (1) Cogan's grocery at No. 10, the entry point for the garrison after the GPO evacuation; (2) Plunkett's butcher shop at No. 16, the last headquarters; and (3) O'Hanlon's fishmongers at Nos 20 and 21, where the rebels were informed of the

surrender by Seán MacDermott. To date, the campaign has succeeded in having the houses accorded National Monument status. Dubbed by some as 'Ireland's Alamo' due to their role in the 1916 Rising, they cannot be touched without ministerial consent. If such consent were to be given, the campaign leaders have pledged to seek an EU ruling to block it.

In recent months Dublin City Council has also passed a motion calling on the government to designate all of Moore Street as a national monument, but ultimately, the recession may have the biggest part to play. Although Chartered Land continues to be supported by the National Asset Management Agency, it seems very unlikely that the new development will be completed by its projected end date of 2016.

As the argument rages, it may seem as though the traders are in danger of being forgotten – a familiar story in the market's long history. If developments get under way there are talks of them being moved temporarily to nearby Wolfe Tone Street and many fear that once that happens they will never be allowed to return. Patrick

Hands around Moore Street protest, April 2009. Over 300 people were required to complete the circuit.
(Courtesy of Photocall Ireland)

Cooney, son of a London East End stallholder and spokesperson for the Save Moore Street Committee, is as much an advocate for the traders as he is for the street he is trying to save. As he points out, both go hand in hand:

> They have been much abused for decades by the city planners. I have always seen them as unpaid ambassadors for the city. It is amazing that they are still there. This sterilisation of the city that the planners cling to is now very dated and has proven to be corrosive in every sense. The notion that somehow supermarkets are more conducive and acceptable than market stalls is laughable. We believe in a forward-thinking, holistic approach. Don't close the market: extend it, weave in workshops, more stalls – add organic value. What we can achieve here has a wider significance. It's about forcing a change, not just in the future of planning, conservation and retail, but in the cultural and social life of the country. The battle for Moore Street is really the battle for Ireland.[162]

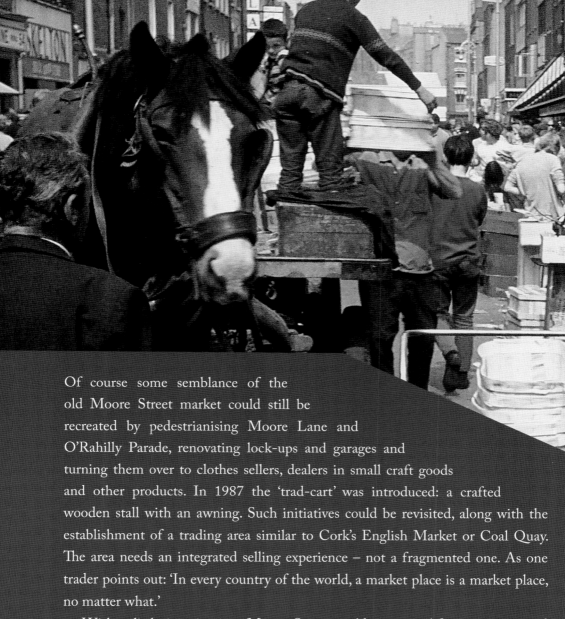

Of course some semblance of the old Moore Street market could still be recreated by pedestrianising Moore Lane and O'Rahilly Parade, renovating lock-ups and garages and turning them over to clothes sellers, dealers in small craft goods and other products. In 1987 the 'trad-cart' was introduced: a crafted wooden stall with an awning. Such initiatives could be revisited, along with the establishment of a trading area similar to Cork's English Market or Coal Quay. The area needs an integrated selling experience – not a fragmented one. As one trader points out: 'In every country of the world, a market place is a market place, no matter what.'

With a little imagination, Moore Street could come to life once again and encouragingly, some positive steps have already been made in that direction. Working with the traders, the Ilac Centre (also owned by Chartered Land) established a committee including the traders in 2007. Having visited a number of international markets, they quickly realised that Moore Street stood alone in its lack of central governance. In Dublin (unlike elsewhere) each trader, regardless of whether they work from a fixed pitch or a pram, pays a rate to the City Council under the terms of the Casual Trading Act – a system that causes them to adopt an

HAIR STYLIST

Unloading on a crowded
Moore Street, *c. 1960.*
(Courtesy of Michael Wood)

individual, rather than a collective approach to selling. In some parts of the market, this has led to a glut of too many people selling the same fruit or vegetable product and diversification is badly needed.

The answer may be to bring in a management agency. These are commonplace in many foreign street markets, where organisation is key to their survival. Representatives police the streets (helping to eliminate counterfeit trade), keep the stalls presentable and assist the traders to diversify into baked goods, dairy, condiments and even craft products.

Another aspect of the plan is to bring the market to life after hours. The metal stalls, which currently lie idle in the street by night and on Sundays, would be removed to a storage area, leaving the street open to continental-style restaurants and cafés. By embracing some of these changes, the traders may end up saving Moore Street themselves.

Part 2:
Voices of Moore Street

May Gorman at her fish stall, *c.* **2006.**
(Courtesy of Eamon Martin)

The Queen

May Gorman

May Gorman (née McGrath), the current Queen of Moore Street, looks much younger than her ninety-one years. Born on the street, her life has been a hard but lively one. She was married twice and had seven children – all home births in tenement rooms, first in Dominick Street and later in Greek Street. 'It's a good day,' she says, 'when you can put your feet to the ground.' She was crowned queen at the tender age of eighty-four in 2005.

I was born at No. 24 Moore Street in 1921. It was the same house that the Lees lived in during the Rising. I heard it from Aunt Hennie [Gorman] that the Kennys wouldn't open the door when The O'Rahilly was shot. He was asking for a drink of water. The Lee brothers opened it for him, and there's a plaque up there now. People used to say things after the Rising. They used to joke about Nannie Dunne's stall, that her husband must have picked up all the sovereigns [from the GPO].

After my mother died, me and my brothers were taken in and reared by my Aunt Hennie at No. 24 Little Denmark Street. Later, when I got married, I got a room for myself in No. 14 Dominick Street. I used to scrub the stairs across the street for a Mrs Malby for a half crown to make ends meet. She used to come down and say, 'You didn't finish a bit, I should have only given you two shillings for that.' I used to wash the steps down outside my room as well – all down the landing. I was reared up doing it. One day, an aul neighbour looked out, and she says, 'What are you doing?' When I explained that I was washing the steps, she said she would have to do something about that, and I ended up not having to pay my five shillings a week rent.

There was a man living at the back of the house called Ban Lasses. He was really just a kind of down-and-out. You'd have to go past him when you went out to the yard. Mrs Hawkins set the rooms and she sort of took pity on him. She allowed him to stay there rent-free if he chopped a bit of wood for her. Well, one morning he woke up in an awful state. 'I heard a bit of a commotion last night Mrs Hawkins,' he says. 'I heard Mr Woods saying, "Oh no, no" and it sounded like Mrs Woods.' Now Mrs Woods had died at the time, and they used to live in the parlour room upstairs – Mr Woods was after having a vision of her, and he fell down the banisters into the basement near where Ban Lasses slept. He was after seeing a ghost of her standing on the landing with her hair all in two long plaits – she pushed him down the stairs and killed him. The dispensary doctor had to come because poor Ban was shaking. The doctor said that was true because Ban was so out of his mind after it. As sure as Jaysus it happened. I tell you no word of a lie.

There used to be wakes that time and you'd make a stew out of fish to give people. I remember one time being at Tommy Sheridan's wake, and when he died his two eyes were open. Imagine a dead person and the two eyes looking at you. Well, someone got two pennies and put them on the eyes. The next thing we looked, the pennies were gone and his eyes was open. Rosie Sheridan said, 'I've no more pennies to put on them eyes!'

I used to go down and help me Aunt Hennie with her stall on the market and that's how I come to work on Moore Street. She sold vegetables – cabbages mostly. Then I had my own stall selling cod, mackerel and whiting, directly across from the house I was born in. I used to get up at four in the morning to be in the [fish] market at five.

Ah, the street was a great place in those days. I used to see Mr Plunkett going up the street in his aul hackney car. Then you had Mrs Kenny, who used to talk real funny to the customers: 'She's looking for veg; she must be making a stew.' When she'd only potatoes left, she'd say, 'There's no veggy today, only all mashy.' At Hallowe'en, the women at the end of the street used to wear big hats – oh, it was a *great* street in those days.

It was hard work too. When it rained, I used to wear a man's soft hat that I got from Mr McGuirk. You'd have to go home and change three times a day it would be that wet out – get into dry clothes and go out and stand on the street again. I remember one of the neighbours went to bed in her kossicks and couldn't get them off her. The cobbler had to come over from Moore Street and cut them off her with a knife, her feet were so swollen.

All the people used to come up from the country of a Holy Thursday. It was all herrings they bought – they'd get us to wrap them up for them while they went down to buy clothes.

I didn't have an easy life in them days at home either. We used to go to the pawn on Dominick Street with a bundle of wet clothes and hand them in to get money for the dinner. They'd smell terrible when you got them out again.

All the scrubbing was done on an aul glass washboard. You'd maybe be washing one child in an iron basin and getting another one ready for Denmark Street School. My first husband was lovely, but the second fella gave me an awful life. 'Hell won't be full till he's in it,' I used to say, 'there won't be enough coal to burn him.'

The air-raid shelters were on the street. One of them was right outside our front door. They were concrete with a door at the front and back. The young people used to go into them when they'd be courting and sometimes in the morning you'd see them coming out. We used to joke that they were only short of having a *bed* in them.

When I started on the street it was during the war years, when things was all rationed. We couldn't get fruit and veg from Little Mary Street. It all came in off the boat at the North Wall. Christy Butler used to go down in his horse and cart to bring up all the stuff. Tea was rationed too. My first husband worked on the docks and he used to rob a load of tea and stuff it into his pockets. You'd nearly have to *bribe* the boss to get a job – the men used to pass a fiver in a box of matches to get one.

At that time they were selling unsalted margarine out of the Colonial Stores on Moore Street, passing it off as butter, but it wasn't the real stuff. They used to use two little paddles and then pound it into the shape of a lump of butter.

I had five children at home in Dominick Street – all home births. After that, I moved to Greek Street and had another two children there. I'm still going strong. I was made the Queen of Moore Street a few years ago by Tony Gregory, Lord have mercy on him, probably because I'm the oldest one there now. The way I look at it, it's a good day when you can put your feet to the ground.

Brendan Egan.
(Author's collection)

The Butcher

Brendan Egan

Brendan Egan (aged eighty) hails from a long-standing butchering tradition. The Wicklow man is proud of his time in the trade. Here he recalls his experiences as a young apprentice, when he cycled into Moore Street from Stillorgan once a week to despatch cattle and sheep.

I come from a family of three brothers and four sisters. My father had a grocery shop in Newtownmountkennedy, County Wicklow, but the others were all butchers. My Uncle Tommy (b. 1895) had a slaughterhouse in Black Pitts. He had come up to Dublin from Athlone in 1911 and served his time in Donnybrook, working with my grandfather. By 1924 he had his own shop. He was the brains of the operation and ended up owning five or six shops.

When I came to Dublin, I started work for Dessie McDonagh in Stillorgan. I used to cycle from there to Moore Street once a week to kill the cattle for a Tipperary butcher named Heron. There were at least thirty-four butchers' shops in Moore Street in those days: McAllister, Buckley, Troy, to name a few. They all started out as open-fronted shops with the slaughterhouses behind them.

We used to have to be up at Manor Street by about 5.30 a.m. The boss would go into some hotel while we started out with the cattle. We used to drive them down to Moore Street. The slaughterhouses was all in terrible condition because at that time there was no such thing as health and safety. The roofs would be leaking.

I used to start by putting a rope on the cattle. There was a ring in every slaughterhouse in the wall – you lassoed the animal and put the rope on it. It would be fairly long, mind you. We used what was known as a humane killer. It was very heavy – about 5 pounds in weight – and when you were killing a bullock you had to press it tight against the forehead. Some of them used to take more than one shot because the skull might be very hard.

I often got a wild Polly [cow] that would smell the blood and many's the time I had to jump up on the windowsill to get out of the way. When they fell down, they usually went down on their forelegs. There was always a porter with you for the next part, and when you pulled the trigger he was trained to roll it over – depending on whether you were left- or right-handed. Then you got the knife, and you put it in the throat and bled the animal. Just at the breast, you shoved a knife in there, and that caused the blood to flow out – the porter would catch the animal by the tail and put his leg on the back hip to pump it. We also used to put a long kind of a cane into a hole in the forehead to clean out the bits of brain – nothing was electrical.

The next part was that you sided off the cattle (put them over on the back). You took apart the legs at the knee cap and put them behind the back leg just to keep everything level. You could only side off so much. Then you got a winch, and you put that into the two back legs, and you hoisted the animal up – that was called backing off. Then you brought it up another 7 or 8 foot and put it up on the rafters, opened it and cleaned it out. The insides would just fall to the ground.

I used to kill about sixty-five ewes on a Tuesday. They were done slightly different. Instead of cutting down towards the heart, we used to cut them straight across the windpipe after shooting them. Cattle were done on a Wednesday, and you might do ten of them. We had contracts for hotels like the Gresham and the Four Courts. You got all those orders done up and got up what those hotels wanted.

The Jews up in Prussia Street were different. They would have a knife with no handle on it called a Kosher knife – it was just a blade. They used to say their prayers over the meat, but they wouldn't shoot it, they would just knock it down. The Irish butchers was always looking to get a job with the Jews because that meant that you didn't have to work of a Saturday [i.e. the Jewish Sabbath].

Some butchers used to be very mean and wouldn't spend their money on the bullets. One butcher used to say, 'It's a waste of bullets. Cut their throat.' I used to do that when I was very young, but you could get into terrible trouble for it. There was a lad caught in Moore Street doing that and he got six months in prison.

It wasn't like it is now. There wasn't much hygiene. We had cold water to wash down the cattle and sheep when we killed them, you couldn't use hot water. We used to take our [butcher's] clothes off us when we would be finished killing on a Wednesday and the same gear would be hanging there until the following Wednesday. Then you just went back down to the sheds and put them on again. A lot of the lads drank very hard – it was a very *hard* life. We'd no conditions, no pensions, nothing.

You had to dress the windows of the butcher's shop on a Friday night. Every shop had to have a display that was different from his competitor's because people window-shopped. It was all about how you laid out the meat: the housekeepers cut, rib on the bone, hand gigots, necks of lamb on trays. Butchering was a great trade then. Buckley's in Moore Street was an open-front shop, but later on they all got windows put in.

During the time of the war, my uncle had three lorries on the road. My eldest brother Ned drove one of them. Then they couldn't get petrol. In 1945 a strike was called because the butchers were looking for a fortnight instead of a week's holiday every year. Our uncles owned the shop so we couldn't participate much in it. The union was very strong then. There was fights, and there was damage done, such as breaking into slaughterhouses and destroying the cattle. Moore Street was a rough place to work in: there was a clique; they were rough men.

Our porter Jimmy used to have the keys of the shop that time and he worked very hard for my uncle. He used to come in every Sunday morning to check the fridges and he would take home some meat. That was his perk. Jimmy went out on strike and all the time Uncle Tommy gave him his full wages – he was very decent with him.

I was staying in digs in Grantham Street for me uncle in Richmond Street, and I went to a dance in South Anne Street one night. I met this girl and took her up for a dance – but it was only lemonade then. She asked me where I was from and she asked me what I was doing in Dublin. 'I'm serving me trade as a butcher,' I said. 'Oh, that's a very good job,' she said. It was very well regarded – better than a plasterer or a carpenter. It did me no harm anyhow. I eventually got married in 1962.

Alice Dardis (née Dunne).
(Courtesy of Sean Girton)

The Stallholder

Alice Dardis

Now eighty years old, Alice Dardis has a strong connection with Moore Street. She sold fish and vegetables there, not far from her hall door at No. 42. She recalls the loyalty her mother held for the street as she walked into the market from Ballybough twice a day to buy her groceries. Later, great excitement heralded the beginning of the dealer of the year competition – a long-standing event on the street.

My mother was reared by a woman in Dominick Street. They all sold in Moore Street. We were brought up first in Sean MacDermott Street, but when I was three years old we moved to a corporation house in O'Sullivan Avenue, Ballybough. My mother still went down to Moore Street twice a day to do her shopping. She wouldn't buy an *egg* in Ballybough – 'Oh, too dear, too dear,' is all she used to say.

The younger ones of our family didn't like going to Moore Street because you'd be sitting at the stall talking to everyone and they wanted to come home. I remember being sent out at eleven or twelve o'clock at night to get messages.

It was a great street. The dealers would all shout across to each other, and they all kept their own surname. If they saw someone walking past dressed a bit funny or having any airs and graces, they'd say, 'Oh, such a body. Did you see her? All fur coat and no drawers!'

A load of cabbage used to come up from the country. It'd be piled up high in the cart and dropped into the street by Paddy Boylan. It cost 30*s* for a load of cabbage. When you were selling well, you'd send down for another one. It's a wonder how the horse made it back home at all. That's when you could call it cabbage – it was lovely.

They used to sell fish from Tuesday to Friday and do the vegetables on Saturday. Monday was the dealers' day off, when they used to dress themselves up and go shopping.

You'd have people coming along at five o'clock when the dealers would be clearing up. They'd take the fish that was left over or a few cabbage leaves. They used to call them the 'pickaroonies'. Most of them had no money, although I knew a man that had a good job down in the court.

I was married in 1956 and lived for three years in Moore Street. I moved into a room above Joe Walsh's pork butchers at No. 42 on the corner of the lane where the clothes sellers lived. We used to have to lift down the banister to get a pram up and down. Me brother had it on a nail, and you could lift it off to take it out of the way.

My window was very small and low to the ground. You could see everything that was going on in the street. I saw a woman one day. They had meat in the window across the street with a door each side. This woman walked in and just took up her meat and walked out again. She was a bit of a wino. A fella ran out after her. She embarrassed him the more he embarrassed her. 'Wait till I get you home. I'll give you what for.' The poor man didn't open his mouth.

There was always a great buzz, especially around 1956 or '58 when the dealer of the year competition started. They ran it at night-time between the dealers. The whole street was lit up, and they put the stalls into the middle of the road to see who would be the Queen. I had a crowd from Ballybough down. Rosie Johnson won it outright. My grandfather who worked in Williams' of Henry Street was very great with her. Every day he used to bring her a bottle of stout.

It was always very hard in the winter, although December was great. Daisy Aiken had a stall down the lane outside her tenement house. During Christmas week she'd take all the toys she had and take them all out to the side of Moore Street to sell them off. The sun never shone on the side of the street I lived on and up until Eastertime you'd freeze with the breeze coming down the lanes. The left-hand side coming in from Parnell Street always got the sun.

Just to be neighbourly I'd bring down a pot of tea for Biddy Hawkins and some of the people that reared me mammy. On a Saturday I'd do a stew.

I always had big legs and I had to get someone to pull the kossicks off me. If you sat at the fire with them on you, it'd scorch the legs off you because they were made of rubber.

When anyone died belonging to the street, the hearse was brought back down, and they'd stop outside where you used to work. You'd be brought around the world before you got to Glasnevin. Back in the days when they used horses the children would all go on the back of them and get a jaunt up to the graveyard.

At night the men used to throw stones at the back at all the rats running across. They used to come down our chimney and everything. In the end, I was taken out of Moore Street and put into Finglas because a rat took the top off my child's soother. But despite it all, it was a great street in its time.

Catherine Hansard.
(Courtesy of Catherine Hansard)

The Hawker

Catherine Hansard

The daughter of a deep-sea docker, Catherine Hansard, mother to singer Glen Hansard, spent much of her childhood growing up in Dublin's Monto in the north inner city. Her working life as a hawker selling off a pram was often tough, but it was interspersed with many lighter moments. As she says herself, 'We were the walking trade, like Molly Malone.'

My father was a deep-sea docker. They gave him his button [guaranteeing him first pick for work over non-regulated men], but he got it too late. When they finally deregulated the button and made them all equal, he was coming out on retirement anyway. He was a very refined aul fella from Kevin Street, who used to walk with a brolly. He always used to keep himself very clean. He'd say, 'If you never have a penny, have your appearance.'

At first, we lived in Mary's Lane down near the fruit market. From there we went into John's Lane and then down to Liberty House – the corporation buildings next to Foley Street. We lived in an area where all the sailors used to frequent. They used to drink in Clare's [pub], but there was an underpass between it and a house of ill repute next door. The madams had gone from Monto at that stage because Frank Duff had got rid of them, but there was one left in the area.

I used to go for all the madam's messages. I used to say to me mammy, 'Oh, she has lovely daughters.' She had lovely gold wallpaper with red velvet designs on it. Mammy would never tell me what the girls were doing, but the madam used to give me *6d* a week for getting their messages during the day. The madam supplied the church with flowers for the Mass on Sunday, and she'd sit there with the beads on her fingers. I used to wonder why me father called her 'a *proper* madam'. But she used to lend money to my mother, and she had henchmen if you didn't pay up. They beat my father to a pulp one time.

We sold off prams with boards on them – we had a hawker's licence. We couldn't park up like the other dealers so we had to keep moving. We used to move out into Henry Street and onto O'Connell Bridge. We were the walking trade, like Molly Malone.

All the fruit and veg was auctioned in the market in those days. What the dealers got for Moore Street was what the shops didn't buy. Someone mightn't give the price for a pallet of tomatoes because they were too ripe, so the street would buy them. We'd buy the whole pallet between us and divide it out. We might get a discount, but we had to take the whole thing. Now there might be four boxes of rotten fruit or veg in that but you had to take the lot. The shops and hotels could examine but we didn't have that luxury. You took pot luck. Sometimes you could get lucky and get a perfect pallet. The auctioneers were very decent though. They used to throw up a box or two to make up the difference.

A joke was told about these three dealers from Moore Street who went into the market one morning, and one of them was deaf. One of them came out and said, 'Jaysus, Maggie, did you see them oranges I got? They're *that* size.' The other one said, 'Would you g'wan out of that, did you see the bananas I got? They're *that* length.' Then the deaf one said, 'I know him. He lives in our flats!'

In October we used to go out with the bangers hidden in our clothes. We were chased by the police more times. I used to bring home the Halloween stuff that was left over. The kids would be waiting at home in Ballymun where I had a flat at the time. Glen thought it was great because his ma was coming with the fireworks – I'd come with the bangers, the star lights, the Catherine wheels and everything. I used to go out on one of the greens in front of the block and we'd let it all off.

We were out in all weathers from half six in the morning, pushing a pram up the street. Rain, snow, it didn't matter – Saturday night up to seven o'clock as well as Christmas Eve; you were constantly standing in damp weather. A lot of the traders died young from that. They were weather-beaten. I remember one woman who was widowed, and she was after having fourteen children. Then she remarried a man with eleven kids. They gave her two flats next door to each other in O'Devaney Gardens and they reared the whole lot of them in those. From giving birth so many times her two hips had gone out, but she was *still* out on Moore Street selling. She used to be in agony in the cold weather.

But as bad as it was for the people selling the fruit and veg, it was ten times worse for the ones that were selling the fish because they had to put their hands down into barrels of ice. It was rough. People got a living out of it, but they all still lived in Monto, Greek Street – places like that. Nobody ever bought a house out of it.

The women used to stand at their stalls with bottles of stout with a glass on top, and they might have a sup of brandy. At night the stall would be packed in, and they'd go into the pub to count all their day's takings, but you never heard of them getting robbed or mugged. They were carrying their profits on them all the time.

My da's mother was a dealer in Camden Street where she had a full licence to sell fruit and veg. We didn't have one for Moore Street in the beginning, although we used to do occasional selling there – there was a protocol down there that that was your spot. Nobody would ever cover it. Then, during the late sixties, a lot of the shops and stalls started shutting down along where the Ilac Centre is now. It became a bit derelict so we made an application for a licence to sell fruit and veg along there.

At Christmas I used to go out into Henry Street. Me mammy would stay on the standing we had in Moore Street and I would sell on Henry Street for this much bigger dealer called Essie Hughes. She had four stalls. I used to have to bring the kids with me. They'd sell the wrapping papers, the Cheeky Charlies and all the mechanicals. They used to wind them up. Afterwards, I'd bring them up to Woolworth's for a cup of tea and a few chips. When we'd close up, they'd push the pram with me up to Chancery Street to Essie.

Essie's house faced the back of the market where the trucks used to drive out. The pram would be full of her stock. One time I put the £750 takings from that day into it. It was just a matter of wheeling it into her gate and leaving it under her sitting-room window. I knocked in and said, 'Everything is there.' She put everything into the stores at the side of her house and left the pram under the window. No one would touch it. It was only an aul Rolls Royce of a thing. The next day was Saturday so me and the kids went back to get the stuff. Glen was playing at the pram. 'Ma, look!' he says. There was the bag of money lying where I had left it all night. It wasn't touched. When we went in and told Essie, she said, 'Oh Sacred Heart of Jaysus! How did you find that?'

'The young fella found it,' I told her. So she went inside and gave him a little twinkle [toy]. She said, 'Give that to your girlfriend.'

The walking trade: Catherine Hansard (*left*)
pictured on a bustling Moore Street.
(Courtesy of Catherine Hansard)

Seanie Lambe.
(Courtesy of Seanie Lambe)

The Community Worker

Seanie Lambe

Seanie Lambe is chairperson of the Inner City Organisations Network (ICON) and director of the Inner City Renewal Group (ICRG). He comes from a family of market traders. During the course of his long career, he has advocated for the rights of market traders both at work and in their own homes.

I was born in 1948. From the time I was six or seven I was going to the market with my father. My grandfather on me father's side was a street trader as well. On that side, the men were the street traders. On me mother's side, it was the women.

My father sold off a handcart. On Saturdays and Sundays he sold fruit. Wednesdays and Fridays were for fish. When he was selling fish, I used to have to meet him down in the fish market because he worked at night-time. Don't ask me when he slept! The market started early because the stuff would come in, generally from Howth, by six o'clock. If you weren't there on time there'd be nothing left. The big shops would buy in bulk, but me father would get a box of ray, a box of cod or smoked cod (if he could get it) and maybe kippers. Then he'd have to gut it and clean it in the house before setting off.

The handcart had huge steel-rimmed wheels. Pushing that full of gear from the fish market to Whitehall, uphill all the way, was an awful job, but Da did that all through the fifties. He wouldn't start selling anything until he got to Whitehall, where he had regular customers. Then he'd go around the houses shouting his wares.

One day, when I was eleven, we were pushing the handcart this hot day. We got to the police station at the corner of Griffith Avenue. Da was pushing the cart and

I had my shoulder to the side of it, helping him to push it up the hill. Suddenly, I coiled up. Me da ran into the station. They rang the ambulance and I was carted to the Mater. I was in there for a couple of weeks with pneumonia. When I got out, me da took sick. He had pleurisy, which he got seven times from being out in the weather. He was put into the *same* bed as I was in, and he was there for another three weeks. Then we went back out grafting. When he came home, I got sick in the middle of the night and they had to carry me up to the Mater again. This time, I had double pneumonia. Would you believe it, I was put into the exact same bed as he was in, in Our Lady's ward. We ended up sharing the same bed between us for about three months!

Da also supplied Wimpy's in O'Connell Street with onions. We used to have to peel four bags of them at home at night. The way to avoid your eyes running was to take the skin off without cutting into it. That way, you didn't cry so much. But the *smell* of them – you'd be reeking of onion because we'd no indoor plumbing. There was four houses, one yard, one tap and three toilets out in the yard, two of which were broken. I used to get up in the morning and have a wash in the cold tap – it didn't matter what the weather was. Now if it was really freezing when we were little, me ma would boil a kettle and pour it into a basin, but when we got older it was the cold water.

My grandmother's name was Mary McCarthy (née Reilly). When she was still in her first marriage to John McCarthy, she progressed from street trading to having a stall in the market. She lost the business during the shelling of the Four Courts. The Free State Army closed down the markets because it was immediately behind it, and all those areas were blocked off. She had just bought a load of oranges and the stall was packed with them. By the time she got back in they were rotten.

Granny was a great businesswoman although she couldn't read. She thought she had money after 1922 because she had given the money to her husband to bank it. Unbeknownst to her, he drank the lot of it. He lost his leg in the Boer War when he was only sixteen. They were taken to the battlefield by train and when they were getting out some eejit slammed the door on it. They had to operate on him nineteen times. Each one took another bit of his leg off, until he ended up with a wooden leg. According to me ma, it drove him crazy. He was an officer in the British Legion afterwards, but at the same time he was hiding guns for Michael Collins. Being in the Legion was a *perfect* cover.

When me grandmother lost her place in the market, she went back to street trading on Dorset Street near where she lived. She had what was called three 'stannins' [standings]. Hers was at the corner of Dorset Street and Gardiner Street, and her daughter-in-law worked one exactly outside the Silk Mills between Gardiner Street and the corner of Hardwicke Street. My aunt Peg, her other daughter, had one right at the top corner of Hardwicke Street.

Granny was arrested a few times for street trading. On one occasion, they sentenced her to three months in prison. She wanted to take that so as she could take a stand in protest, but someone paid her fine. She never wanted it to be paid so as she could make an issue of it. Another time, she had her cart with all the gear in it thrown up in the truck behind her and straight down to Fitzgibbon Street police station. She got out the next day and the cart was given back to her. A gun was still underneath where she had hidden it. There was one guy who lived on Synnott Place, and when the Brits would go in to try and catch him he'd go straight over the wall into me granny's. She used to hide him.

She lived in a laneway called Dorset Avenue, and had what you might call an inner-city farm. She had pigs, horses, chickens and geese. She'd buy bonhams [young pigs] in the market and keep them for a year. When we finished school, we had to go out collecting feed and bedding for them.

Me uncle used to bring the produce up to Dorset Street by horse and cart. He also did the buying and selling of the pigs. He died very young, but me grandmother kept that going for a few years afterwards before packing it in. The sties were still there until the houses were knocked down in the seventies.

The conditions out selling in all weathers were horrific back then, but we didn't know it was so bad. It was all we knew. I swore blind I was never getting into it so as soon as I could I got a job in the *Independent*.

During the 1980s pressure was being put on the traders by the City Centre Business Association. The women that they targeted were only hawkers – traders who sold boxes of bananas, flowers, chocolate or jewellery from a pram. At the instigation of the Association, the police used to bring them down to Store Street.

Afterwards, they'd let them out but keep their stuff. If a woman was selling daffodils, she might go back on the Monday and they'd be all dead. A lot of them did time.

In 1986 Tony Gregory, Christy Burke and Joe Costello got involved because a lot of the women were from this area. They sat down in a protest in O'Connell Street but Tony and Christy got lagged. Tony spent four days in prison for it.

When a new rainbow coalition came into power in 1994, Pat Rabbitte got a job as minister for state at the Department of Enterprise and Employment. They started to draw up legislation to introduce huge fines for street trading – £6,000 for women trying to earn an honest living. I brought a gang of them over to meet Pat at the Department of Enterprise in Kildare Street. When we arrived, Pat brought in the two guys who were framing the legislation – civil servants. Then he disappeared for an hour. They had as much sympathy for these women as they

From left to right, front row: **Seanie Lambe, Bernie Murphy, Joanna Rooney, Mary Rooney (seated), Lillie Murphy, —;** *back row:* **Bridget Meyler, Chrissie Mangan, Lillie O'Driscoll, Mary Donnelly** (*c.* 1994).

(Courtesy of Seanie Lambe)

had the man on the moon. They were technocrats and didn't want to know about our problems.

I knew the legislation was designed to catch the likes of guys in Hiaces that were buying washing machines for half nothing in Northern Ireland and bringing them down for sale in street markets with no tax paid. But it meant that our women were being affected as well. I told them, 'Look, if you give a woman a fine of £6,000, how do you think she's going to raise it? She'll have to do more street trading!' It made no sense whatsoever. Talk about using a sledge hammer to crack a nut. These women wouldn't even earn that money in a year.

We thought we made a very strong case, but the government insisted on completing the legislation – no doubt at the behest of the City Centre Business Association. But they put a get-out clause in it: the legislation had to be triggered by the local authority. They never initiated it, but on the other hand I've never heard of it being repealed. It was *absurd*.

In step – Stevo Lynch (Snr) with his horse Dolly on Moore Street.
(Courtesy of Stevo Lynch)

The Delivery Man

Stevo Lynch Junior

*S*tevo Lynch, son of the legendary 'Stevo', has now retired, but not so long ago he worked as one half of a father-and-son team, delivering fruit and vegetables to Moore Street on a daily basis. As he says himself, 'The cart was the dealers' lifeline – an artery from the market to the street.'

Me granddad Paddy Lynch started it all. He started in Moore Street with a handcart and progressed from that to a horse. Me father came on the scene when he was about sixteen years of age. He took over from his father when he went to Birmingham.

We had a stable and yard on Henrietta Lane. The granddad bred pigs there and kept five or six horses. He used to make the pig swill in a big barrel buried in the ground. He'd get the best of gear to make that up: potato peels and bits of meat from behind the slaughterhouses. On a freezing cold morning, it would be smelling lovely. Before starting out for the market, they'd put their cups into it and scoop it out. It's a wonder the pigs got any of it.

By the time I came along, we had three horses. We had to use Irish draught animals. Elvis was our piebald stallion and he used to eat the apples off the stalls. One day, one of the dealers on the street says, 'Go wan out of that Elvis' and the name stuck. After that, the last horse we had was a grey mare called Dolly. To start with we had to bring her around the city to get her used to sounds because it was important that she wouldn't be afraid of traffic. We used to try her out first on a Sunday when it wasn't too busy. You'd have to coax her and keep her calm.

One day Dolly got spooked and Da had to take her back up to the yard to calm her down. We were left with a cartload of gear and no horse to take it from the market. I got between the shafts with one of the lads pushing behind me with a forklift. Once I took the end of the shafts, there was no weight in it and no problem steering it. By the time we got as far as Bolton Street, it was lunch hour. One of the students shouted, 'Hey mister, were you on the Guinness last night?' It clicked with me then. Hey, he's right. This *is* like the Guinness ad!

Dolly had a brake fitted: a big leather strap at her backside. When she stopped, that stopped the cart from hitting her directly, but I'll never forget the day it snapped. The cart came forward and she bolted. Me and me da jumped off, and she flew down Parnell Street. She was on the path beside the Ilac Centre with the cart knocking down every pole. There was a woman going into the centre car park. The cart went straight into her car and got embedded in it. We thought she was dead, everything was that badly smashed up. The ambulance and fire brigade had to come down. The horse broke loose then and bolted. I ran up the street after her, but it was pointless. There was no way you'd catch her.

The next thing that happened, she got just up to Smyth's toy store where the cars were coming out. I thought she was going to get a smack of a car. But the traffic lights went red. On me mother's life, she *stopped*. I couldn't believe it. Over the years, she had been watching the lights all the time. She mightn't know the colours but if she saw them changing, she knew to stop. Only for that, she would have been killed.

Every day we started work at five o'clock in the morning. Me da used to yoke up the horse and cart, which took a good twenty minutes. He always took the reins but he never wore gloves. Because he was holding the reins all them years, his hands got shaped from it.

We'd go straight to the market and load up for the dealers in Moore Street. That was grand once we had the forklift, but previous to that me da had to handball everything, box by box. I'd stack all the stuff for individual dealers on one pallet and wrap it to keep it separate. As soon as the car was full to the brim, we'd start off. On a busy day, we'd do about four to five runs. May Gorman or one of the other dealers could be selling well and run out of stock. We might oblige them during the day by bringing up a tray of fish or pallet of fruit.

In the evening time, we used to take the stuff around to the lock-ups behind the street. The principle was that you pulled the oldest produce out to the front, but we used to go in there during the summer and, my Jaysus, the heat would hit you – you better believe it. The stuff would be gone off in no time.

Me da used to sit on a milk crate. Under that we'd have the bits and pieces in case we got punctures. With a full load, there's nothing as bad as a puncture. We had incidents where the pallets would fall off. Imagine trying to pick up all of that – oranges and apples with cars going over it.

We used to finish up about 12 p.m. Then we'd make our way back to the yard, unyoke the horse, put on her little jacket and leave her to have a run around the yard. Me father would do his book then. She'd walk into that stable herself; no problem. As soon as he'd clean it out and put the food in for her, she'd go in. She'd come in behind you but there wasn't much room to manoeuvre. If you weren't looking out, she'd hit you against the wall. Many's the time you'd have to go under her just to go out.

Da wouldn't get paid until that Saturday. He went from dealer to dealer to settle up. He was paid by carriage [per box] but every so often, when a big pallet came down, he would use his own initiative and price the whole pallet, rather than count every item in it.

He never missed a day's work in his life. Even if there was a funeral, he'd only go to it after the best part of the work was done and he'd come back afterwards. Rain, hail or snow, he went out. There was no calling in sick. Sure who would you ring in to? Ring the *horse* and say 'I'm not coming in'? The cart was the dealers' lifeline – an artery from the market to the street. If Stevo wasn't in, it was a domino effect.

Then things started getting slack and we went down to one horse. Me father finished five years ago. They had a little surprise party for him. After that we sold the horse and everything in the stable. The market is totally different now. Me father went down to visit Moore Street a few weeks ago. I said, 'What did you think of it?'

'Do you know what?' he says, 'I seen one or two faces that I knew, but there's more empty stannins down there than there's full ones now.'

We had great days down there, but it's something that you'll never see again. It's the end of an era.

P. J. Gallagher.
(Courtesy of the Lisa Richards Agency)

The Comedian

P. J. Gallagher

M oore Street and its traders have provided inspiration to countless comedians. From Jimmy O'Dea's 'Biddy Mulligan' to Brendan O'Carroll's 'Mrs Brown', the area continues to breed life into new characters. Here, P. J. Gallagher talks about the Dirty Aul Wan, visiting the area as a child and the changes he has witnessed in the market over recent years.

Dublin is famous for its sense of humour. The reason there's a Dirty Wan, a Mrs Brown and all those characters is because of Moore Street. That's where it all started, but in the beginnin' the idea for the Dirty Aul Wan was an accident. We had a load of set-ups done for some other character but it all fell through and we were really stuck. We had a big bag of clothes that we used for all the characters. We found all these 'aul wan' clothes in it. One of my mates was poncy enough to have a pair of Ugg boots – even though he was a grown man. That gave us a laugh for a start. So I stuck the clothes on and rolled down his Ugg boots to make them look like aul granny ones and went up Moore Street.

The first thing that came to mind was how uncomfortable it can be for women. They're constantly getting hit on by fellas, but if it went the other way, with an aul wan who looked as if she'd give as good as she got, they wouldn't know what to think of themselves – and they didn't!

Normally, most of the characters we did would take five days of filming with a hit rate of about one in thirty. Afterwards, we'd pick one workable five-minute gag out of that. But with the Dirty Aul Wan, the normal rules just didn't apply. We did it for one whole day and got a *whole series* out of it. We just went from the top of the street to the bottom, stopped as many people as we could and every one of the gags worked.

Of course the dealers were all mad for wind-ups anyway. You'd stop one dealer, do a gag with her and she'd say, 'Go over there and get her. She'd be mad for it.' Then you'd go and do another one and be told, 'Don't be talking to me, would you go over get that one. She's a bit of gas.' But at the same time, I think there was a reverse wind-up going on, the way they got me to talk to some people – 'Get off the street ya *dirt* bird,' one fella said, 'I'll take the head off ya!' I never knew Moore Street had a manager until then.

Moore Street was the only place that we could actually do the same wind-ups to the same woman, two years in a row – that was Bernie. Patrick went up to her and says, 'You're selling illegal prescription sunglasses.'

'Me?' she says. 'I'm not selling prescription sunglasses. Get out of it ya thick.'

We came back the following year, and Jake gets her a second time. 'Hiya Bernie,' he says, 'I hear you're doing a good deal on prescription glasses.'

I don't think you'd have got away with that anywhere except for Smithfield or Moore Street. As a kid, I remember going to get my shoes at the back of the Ilac Centre. Everyone knew someone who knew someone else. You'd get a tip-off: 'Go up there and tell Mary that Josie sent you.' So you'd go up and try the sellers on, but when you're young you're terrible at the bartering. Mary'd say, 'Don't worry, we'll look after you. Give that lad back fifty pence – but not that one, that's a Millennium 50p.'

The sad thing about the street now is that it's on the way out. We could even see that during the three years we filmed there. The first year we did it, it was boom time when all the Paddies were still waiting for Saturday to buy their organic produce from some 'Farmer Joe Smith' who had a great market in Killiney. But the Polish and Latvians, on the other hand, were looking for bargains and that's what brought them down to Moore Street. Bar the odd student who was probably wandering around lost, with a hangover, it was all Eastern Europeans. Nowadays, the street is as international as a Benetton ad.

One of the dealers died during the time we were filming and no one would take over the stall. In days gone past, the stalls were nearly handed down, but now there's no one replacing the owners. But you don't have to look too far to see what it used to be. Now it's like Custer's last stand – the last stand of the aul wan!

(Courtesy of the Lisa Richards Agency)

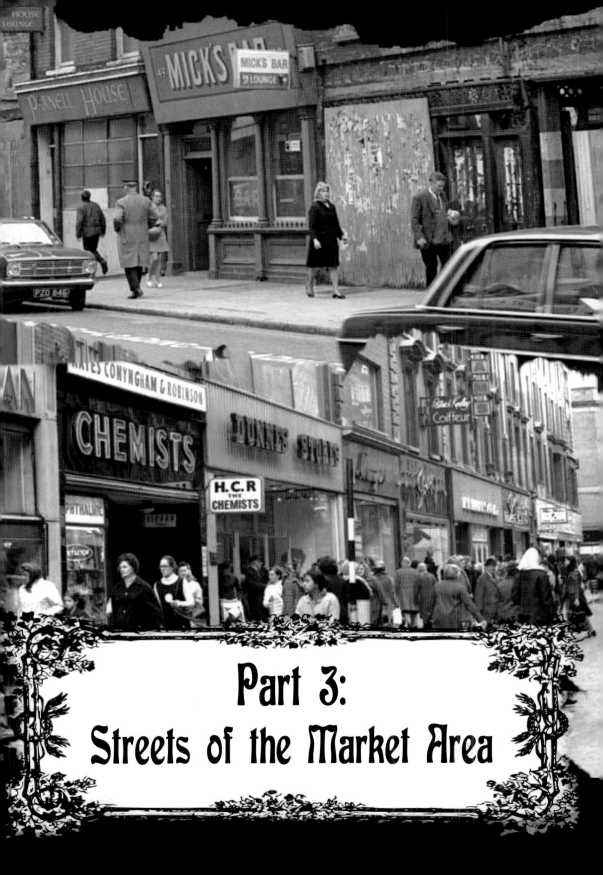

Part 3:
Streets of the Market Area

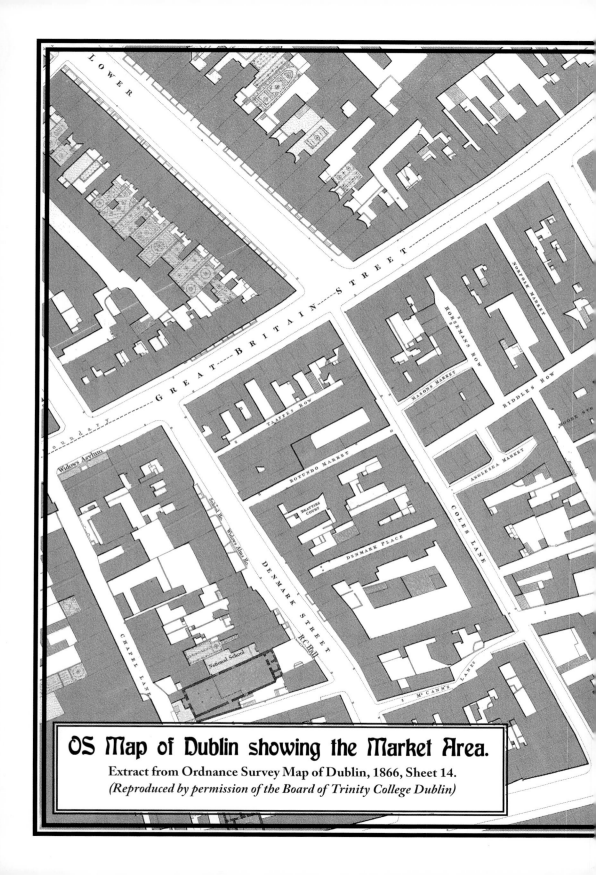

OS Map of Dublin showing the Market Area.

Extract from Ordnance Survey Map of Dublin, 1866, Sheet 14.
(Reproduced by permission of the Board of Trinity College Dublin)

Anglesea Market, *c.* 1900.
(Reproduced by permission of the Royal Society of Antiquaries of Ireland)

The market adjoining Moore Street was a close-packed warren of eighteenth-century alleys and lanes. Among them slaughterhouse men, used-clothes vendors and furniture dealers could all be found plying their trade. It was a busy commercial district, bounded by the fashionable Henry and Parnell Streets, but it was also one of the city's oldest tenement quarters. Such vibrant market life amid an atmosphere of decay captured the attention of many twentieth-century artists, including Tom Cullen, Flora H. Mitchell and Liam Martin, but by the late 1960s what remained of the area was scheduled for demolition. Today, the Ilac Centre stands on the site, leaving little to remind visitors of a once thriving market – a lifeline to generations of Dubliners.

Anglesea Market

This market, established in 1826, was most likely named after Richard, 6th Earl of Anglesea (1694–1761), who held the governorship of County Wexford before 1745. During the second half of the nineteenth century, one of the largest landlords in Anglesea Market was carpenter and town councillor John French (d. 1881), who owned six properties there.[1]

Anglesea Market was known for its small game. The larger stallholders offered hampers to prospective rabbit suppliers, and by the 1870s some of these businesses were selling at least 200 animals a week.[2]

During the Second World War traditions at the market began to change, as custom declined. The pre-war boom gave way to a period of relative quiet, with local stallholders opting to send their children to the technical schools or into shop jobs. Tom Cullen's painting of the lane from 1977 depicts a quiet, flagged thoroughfare with a number of slatted, wooden lock-up facilities. When Dublin historian Éamonn MacThomáis took a stroll through the street during the 1970s, he noted 'the last tattered remains' of Anglesea Market.[3] By then, business was still going on, but was due to come to an end with the scheduled demolition of the buildings in the area and the construction of the proposed Ilac Centre over the site of the old market.

Beattie's Court

This small court was situated just off Rotunda Market. It is depicted on Ordnance Survey maps from the mid nineteenth century onwards. The map for 1847 shows some houses on the northern side of the court with high steps leading up to them.[4]

Bell's Alley

This blind-ending little thoroughfare ran off Market Street (Fountain Row). It was named after Francis Bell, a principal landlord in the area. Bell was married to Anne, the eldest daughter of James Riddall, in St George's Church on 1 April 1824.

Cad's Lough

This interestingly titled alley was located off Sackville Lane. It is listed on a series of Ordnance Survey maps from 1846 onwards. Cad's Lough may once have formed part of a low meadow ground in this area, contiguous with the brickfields of Moore Lane. John DeCourcy notes that brickfields were usually located around clay deposits which, after extraction, became water-logged pits.[5] By the mid nineteenth century, Cad's Lough comprised five two-storey tenement houses. Nos 1 and 2 abutted the rear of 66 Parnell Street. During the 1930s a Mrs Edwards ran a small cake and chocolate shop there.

Chapel Lane

This thoroughfare still exists as a rather long, nondescript street behind the Ilac Centre. It used to lead southwards from Great Britain (Parnell) Street, before turning east to meet Little Denmark Street just past St Saviour's School. The bend in the street is preserved but is now cut off in its course by the rear of the shopping complex. It is clearly marked on John Rocque's map of 1756.

Rocque's map mentions the existence of a 'widow's almshouse' which was built by Tristram Fortick in 1755. Until that period, the lane was known simply as 'Stable Lane'.[6] It was here that the original Penal Day Orphanage of the Dominicans was located, housed in a disused stables. It catered for twenty-five children.[7]

John Rocque's 1756 map.

In 1872 Chapel Lane was the venue for a meeting of the International Working Men's Association. The association was formed in London in 1864 after the suppression of the January Uprising in Poland, where thousands of largely working-class men rebelled against their attempted conscription into the Russian army. One of the association's aims was to establish a powerful lobby group that could operate across national boundaries in the interest of protecting workers' rights. About fifty men attended the meeting on 3 April 1872, but it was disrupted by an unruly mob of butchers' porters from the market:

> Every single article that was in the place and portable was flung about the room and out into the Lane. Mr McKeon said he'd preserve order or perish in the attempt, however he got a blow of a chair and was silenced, the Secretary was struck with another missile full in the face from the effects of which his nose and lips became swollen to the dimensions of a small loaf.[8]

Until the mid twentieth century, Chapel Lane was also home to some factories, as well as a snooker-table manufacturer named Borris & Watts. Underneath the street ran a number of spirit stores owned by the Jameson Distillery.[9] The whiskey was

This old warehouse is one of the last old buildings remaining on Chapel Lane.
(Author's collection)

kept in them for five or ten years before being opened – an event that excited no small amount of curiosity.

The lane also housed the laboratory of the Apothecaries Hall which fronted onto Henry Street. Lectures were delivered there on chemistry and pharmacy, with the aim of producing qualified apothecaries.[10]

Clarke's Court (Coal Yard or Campbell's Ground)

The entrance to this short alley is still located between Nos 4 and 5 Moore Street. From there, it used to swing north onto Mulligan's Lane, a short thoroughfare that opened onto Off Lane (Henry Place). During the late eighteenth century it was known simply as the 'Coal Yard' or 'Campbell's Ground'.[11] By the mid nineteenth century it comprised five small cottages and a yard. In more recent times it has been used as a storage area by Moore Street traders.

Cole's Lane

Cole's Lane is clearly marked as such on John Rocque's map of 1756. Prior to the construction of the Ilac Centre, it extended from the corner of Henry Street to Parnell Street. It was named after Mary Cole (d. 1726), Countess of Drogheda through her marriage to Henry Hamilton Moore, 3rd Earl of Drogheda (d. 1714). Today, only the Henry Street end remains.

During the early eighteenth century, George Simpson established a sugar house on Cole's Lane. An interesting account is given by his gardener, Nicholas Mooney. 'Here it was that I first got an Insight into the Art of Sugar baking,' he writes. 'After a Stay of about three Quarters of a Year here, I was discharged from my Service for staying out all Night at a House of ill fame.'[12]

During the eighteenth century, Cole's Lane was quite affluent, with a number of coach-makers choosing to locate their businesses there. The Earl of Blessington owned some property on the lane. Famous visitors included the opera singer Fedele Rossellini, who lodged at Mrs Fleming's during the summer of 1770.[13] Another renowned resident was William Ogilvie (d. 1832), who kept a school in Cole's

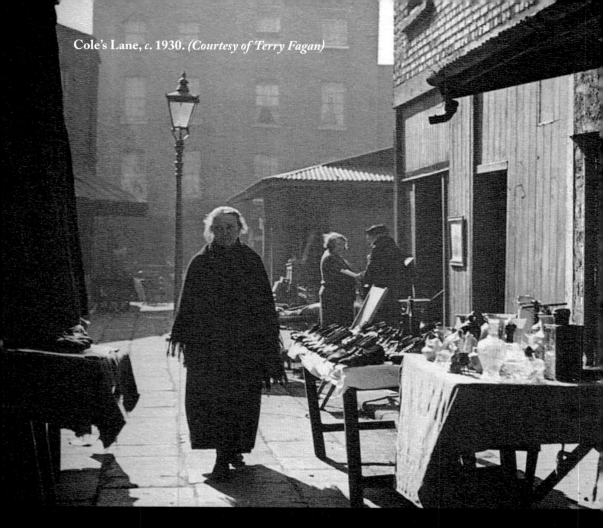

Cole's Lane, *c.* 1930. *(Courtesy of Terry Fagan)*

Lane during the early 1770s. He tutored the sons of Emily Fitzgerald, Duchess of Leinster. They later married in 1774 and had four children together.[14]

By the 1780s butchers were beginning to set up stalls in Cole's Lane, but their arrival was not without controversy, as attested to by Andrew Kippis:

> Yesterday a great number of armed men went to the market in Cole's Lane, and took from thence a butcher, and was bringing him for the purpose of tarring and feathering, when Alderman Hamilton got information, and instantly pursued them; on his appearing they immediately dispersed, without performing their intention. The crime they charged him with was for not serving a regular apprenticeship.[15]

Cole's Lane in the 1940s. *(Courtesy of Pat Clifford)*

The lane once again came to notice in 1797, when a local baker named Segrave was arrested on suspicion of being a United Irishman.[16] His arrest was a foretaste of things to come. When rebellion broke out in 1798, more market traders were arrested.[17] The matter came to a head on 10 June when 'sixty Butchers of Cole's Lane Market took the Oath of Allegiance before Mr. Justice Godfrey, and gave up three of their Leaders, whom they were with difficulty restrained from tearing to pieces, and who are now in confinement'.[18] The prisoners were held at the old Custom House across the River Liffey. During Robert Emmet's rebellion of 1803, a contingent of pikemen was kept in readiness near Cole's Lane in the event of an attack.[19]

The principal landlord of Cole's Lane at that time was Alderman John Cash. In 1800 he ordered twenty-four new houses to be built, each constructed from grey stock bricks with struck ashlar finishing. All of the carpentry was carried out by

Hugh Wooldridge, who, besides fitting architraves and window frames, constructed new shopfronts as well as meat racks for two butchers' premises using 'wrought scantling'. Large, moulded show boards were placed at both ends for advertisement purposes. Where possible, pre-existing infrastructure, such as an old fountain and outdoor privies, were cleaned up, painted and reused.[20]

By 1828 the lane had become known as 'Cole's Alley', a reflection perhaps of its declining stature as a residential street. The butchers were now working alongside a thriving poultry market.[21] An advertisement printed in *The Freeman's Journal* of 18 December 1841 lists a range of livestock for sale, including chickens, ducks, pigeons, turkeys and geese. Rabbits were also sold for 1*s* 8*d* or 2*s* for a pair. No. 11 Cole's Lane specialised in selling sauces made by a London-based company named Bowling, Walker & Co. These included pickle, lobster, shrimp and tomato varieties.[22]

By 1911 over a quarter of the city's second-hand clothes traders could be found on Cole's Lane.[23] The garments were brought there by 'tuggers' – mostly women who trekked out to the affluent suburbs every day, going door to door with wheeled wicker baskets to ask for footwear, clothing and other items. On arrival, they were piled in mounds as high as six feet, cleaned and patched up for resale.[24] A number of the city's open-car drivers owned stables on the lane during this period, and it was also home to a medical dispensary.

Many of the buildings at the Henry Street end of Cole's Lane were destroyed by fire during the 1916 Rising. In its aftermath, the authorities took the opportunity to widen its entrance, but the work did not extend past the Sampson's Lane junction. As a result, the lane assumed a somewhat bottlenecked appearance.[25]

Denmark Place

Denmark Place ran from Little Denmark Street to Cole's Lane. During the early part of the nineteenth century it was home to Lyle Acheson, a member of the Royal Irish Academy. He held the post of Second Remembrancer – a subordinate office of the English Exchequer.[26]

The lane was most noted for its blacksmith forges and cooperage, but by 1850 ten of the houses had become tenements. A number of newspaper reports for the

Denmark Place, c. 1900. *(Reproduced by permission of the Royal Society of Antiquaries of Ireland)*

1870s detail the exploits of Margaret Rickards who kept a house of 'ill fame' there. Denmark Place continued to exist up until the Second World War, but by the late 1940s it had been completely obliterated by a plant yard and machinery showroom owned by Hendron Brothers.

Griffith's Court

This little cluster of houses is marked clearly on the Ordnance Survey map for 1847. It was located near the junction of Moore Lane and Off Lane (Henry Place).[27] Nos 14 and 15 Moore Street backed onto it.

Henry Place (Off Lane)

This thoroughfare is listed on John Rocque's map of 1756 as 'Off Lane', possibly taking its name from the 'of' in 'Henry Moore, Earl of Drogheda'. It runs from Henry Street to Moore Street and is mentioned in the city watch minute book of St Thomas' Parish of 1763. *Thom's Directory* for 1842 lists an interesting mix of businesses including an instrument-maker, a smith and a mat-maker. The houses, all of which were tenements, were home to animal skinners who worked in the nearby

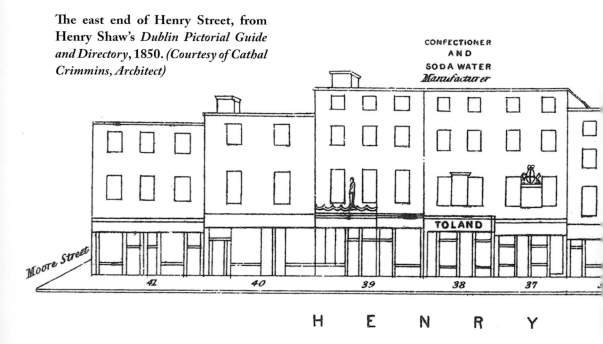

The east end of Henry Street, from Henry Shaw's *Dublin Pictorial Guide and Directory*, **1850.** *(Courtesy of Cathal Crimmins, Architect)*

markets. Some sold 'teetotal refreshments' such as spruce and ginger beer. They drew their water from a public fountain installed at the Moore Lane junction.[28]

Off Lane afforded access to the extensive garden of the Cow Pock Institution, opened on 14 January 1804. Children of the poor were entitled to be vaccinated free of charge there on Tuesdays and Fridays between eleven and three o'clock.[29] The lane was also home to St Mary's Dispensary, established in 1836 under the provisions of the Poor Law Act. It provided relief to those in the parish who had fallen on hard times. On 5 February 1841, *The Freeman's Journal* mentions a visit by the guardians to the dispensary 'for the purpose of making inquiry into the state of the institution'.

During the early Victorian period, Off Lane, with its shebeens and houses of ill-repute, was frequented by sailors. This was a source of concern to the authorities and, as a result, the lane was frequently raided. On 27 March 1866 a letter-writer to *The Freeman's Journal* described the scene that took place every Sunday near the Henry Street end: 'Troops of seamen, without fear or shame, parade themselves and the unfortunates to the public gaze, collecting crowds of lookers-on, disgusting the old, and, I fear, corrupting the young, and bringing shame and sorrow to every respectable resident near them.'

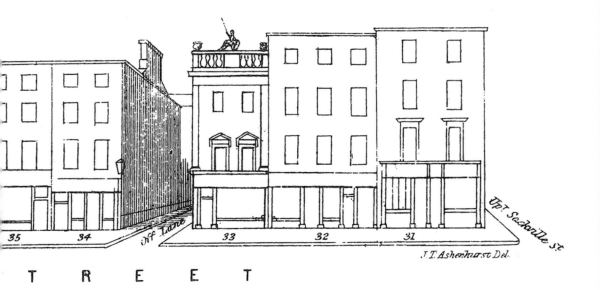

In November 1871, a Swedish sailor stabbed five people in a brawl on Moore Street.[30] Such incidents served to galvanise public opinion. When a private speculator bought a large number of the decrepit buildings in Off Lane in 1872, several of the inhabitants petitioned Dublin Corporation to change its name to 'Henry Place'.

Henry Street

This thoroughfare, which runs from the junction of O'Connell Street to Jervis Street, was once part of the lands of St Mary's Abbey. It is named after Viscount Henry Moore, 1st Earl of Drogheda (d. 1675), who bought the land in 1614. A century later it was sold on to Luke Gardiner.

The first houses were built around 1714. On John Rocque's map of 1756, Henry Street is shown as fully developed, the predominant housing style being curvilinear gable-fronted Dutch 'Billies'. In 1782 the corporation ruled that 'a jut out window

The east end of Henry Street, from Henry Shaw's *Dublin Pictorial Guide and Directory*, 1850. (*Courtesy of Cathal Crimmins, Architect*)

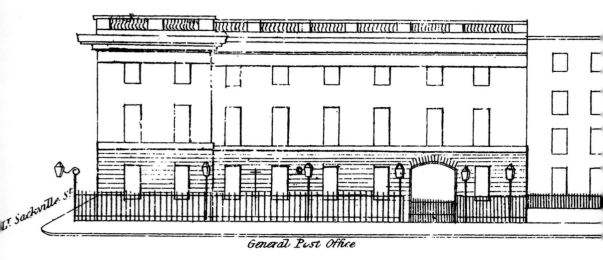

erected in Henry Street, opposite Moore Street, which projects 10 inches' be brought in line with the surrounding buildings.[31]

Notable residents included Robert Stewart (later Viscount Castlereagh; 1769–1822), who was born at his grandfather's house at No. 28.[32] In 1818 Henry Grattan was forced to take refuge in a house on Henry Street after he and fellow parliamentarian Robert Shaw were attacked by a crowd protesting against window and typhus taxes.[33]

By the mid nineteenth century the street was home to sixty-two businesses. Over a quarter of these were involved in woodcraft. They included cabinet-makers, upholsterers and fine carvers. In 1843 a department store named Cannock & White (later Arnott & Co.) was founded at No. 14. However, from the late eighteenth century the rising cost of rent set a trend, with smaller grocery concerns being forced off the street into the burgeoning Moore Street market area.[34]

A number of imposing buildings once graced Henry Street. These included Ball's Bank, near the GPO, with its fittings of Santo Domingo mahogany, and the adjacent Coliseum Theatre, built in 1913. No. 8 housed the office of the city watch and, from 1837, the premises of the Dublin Metropolitan Police.

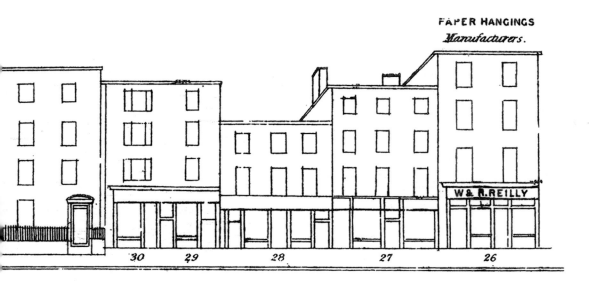

This dining room was erected for Messrs Arnott & Co. on Henry Street in 1875. The architect was George Beater (from *Irish Builder*, Vol. XVII, no. 366, 15 March 1875).

Marks & Co., No. 37 Henry Street.
(Dixon slide collection, courtesy of Dublin City Library and Archive)

In 1894 Nos 11–15 Henry Street were destroyed by fire. The *Evening Mail* of 4 May reported that the blaze was so intense that about 500 soldiers were drafted in from Ship Street Barracks to assist the fire service. Soon afterwards the premises were rebuilt to the design of George Beater. Arnotts, which now comprises Nos 7–15, survived the 1916 Rising, as did No. 6. For the most part, however, the street was rebuilt after 1916 – the buildings comprising concrete faced with red brick. A classical style was favoured, incorporating two-tier oriels and superimposed pilasters. City architect Horace O'Rourke was responsible for planning the design of the ground-floor shops.[35] Another post-Rising architect was Francis Bergin of Westmoreland Street, who had been involved in many renovation projects on Henry Street prior to the Rising. In some instances, he found himself returning to rebuild the same buildings he had constructed prior to 1916. A unified commercial strip was achieved, and it remains one of the longest in the city centre, despite recent developments which have served to erode the elegance of its style somewhat, with the imposition of box-like structures along the northern side of the street.

A lady walks down Horseman's Row in the direction of Parnell Street. Note how the buildings are propped up to prevent collapse.

(Courtesy of Dublin City Library and Archive)

Horseman's Row

Horseman's Row ran from Parnell Street and was intersected by Riddall's Row and Mason's Market. This row was named after a coachbuilder called Martin Horseman, who built a house there in 1803. He started his career as a herald painter and by the 1840s had become a wealthy coachbuilder with a home in Artane. He married Mary Cox in 1820, their marriage settlement entitling him to continue to collect rent on her 'several houses, tenements and premises' so long as he remained solvent.[36] He had a son who was also named Martin.

Thom's Directory for 1842 shows that at that point the street was dominated by provision shops and greengrocers. No. 49, at the Parnell Street end, was a three-storey public house known locally as 'Mick's Bar'. It had an entrance into Horseman's Row, and was defined as a 'typical Joycean tavern' in *Seven Days in Dublin* by Endymion.[37] During the mid nineteenth century it may have been the location of Hart's Rooms, described in many newspaper reports as the venue from which the ballot was counted to decide the return of Poor Law guardians. Inside, intricate wooden carvings behind the bar held spirit bottles in place. The pub was said to be at least 200 years old and was supposedly frequented by Michael Collins during the War of Independence. A secret room was purportedly found there in 1950 by publican Jim Nolan. The room, from which a gun and secret papers were recovered, could only be reached by a narrow staircase.[38] In 1964 the Parnell Street frontage collapsed, but it continued to trade as a one-storey building for another decade or so.

Kane's Court

This thoroughfare, which still exists, is marked on a series of Ordnance Survey maps from 1846 onwards. It runs south off Sampson's Lane and was once known as 'Kane's Court West' to distinguish it from another street of the same name near Gloucester (now Sean MacDermott) Street. It was most likely named after Robert John Kane (1809–90), an Irish chemist whose home at No. 48 Henry Street backed onto it.[39] Kane helped to found the *Dublin Journal of Medical Science* and was elected to the Royal Irish Academy in 1832. He also participated in a commission

National Commissioner for Education (1873) and first Chancellor of the Royal University of Ireland (1880).

Little Denmark Street

Demolished to make way for the Ilac Centre, Little Denmark Street, once known as 'Upper Liffey Street', is depicted on John Rocque's map of Dublin of 1756. Roughly the same width and length as Moore Street, it ran between the top of Henry Street and Parnell Street. One or two buildings predated Rocque's map – in particular a widows' almshouse and parish school. Around the early 1770s it was renamed, possibly after Caroline Matilda, who was a daughter of the Prince of Wales and also Queen of Denmark and Norway by marriage.

At that time the northern end of the street was at the heart of the city's trade and commerce. It was situated near the old Custom House as well as being near a major route into the city. Warehouses lined the thoroughfare, many of which had strong windlasses for hauling bales and barrels, and there were substantial vaulted rooms underneath for storage. At the Henry Street end the buildings gave way to a series of plots or gardens.

A century later the character of the street had changed dramatically. After the relocation of the Custom House, Little Denmark Street was colonised by shoemakers and furniture-brokers. *Thom's Directory* of 1842 also lists a vintner, a coach-builder, a baker and a dressmaker. Other businesses provided goods to the local almshouses.[40] By the turn of the twentieth century there was a significant Jewish community there, with names such as 'Eliassoff' featuring alongside more Irish-sounding ones such as 'Merrigan'.[41]

One of the most distinctive structures on Little Denmark Street was the Dominican Chapel, erected in 1835 to replace an old building that stood at the rear of an old house. During the late eighteenth-century, a chapel had existed to the rear of the same site. It was accessible via an underground passage and was designed to circumvent restrictive penal laws which forbade Roman Catholic worship. In 1798 some of its priests had a part to play in fomenting rebellion. The *London Observer* of 3 June reported that a large number of pikes had been found concealed

Denmark House – an early twentieth-century steel-framed building demolished in 1976 to make way for the Ilac Centre development. *(Courtesy of the Irish Architectural Archive)*

DENMARK
HOUSE

in coffins kept on the premises. A government spy reported that 'a party of priests, McMahon of Denmark Street at their head, meet once or twice a week at Herbert's Tavern, in Clontarf'. A second priest, Fr James Bushe, was arrested in the courtyard while reading his office. Both ended up leaving the country – the first voluntarily to America, the second by transport to Botany Bay.[42]

In 1861 the Dominican order moved to Dominick Street, leaving the building to become St Saviour's School and Orphanage. It was known locally as Scoil Naomh Slánaitheora. The girls and infants entered through a high wall topped by railings on the Denmark Street side, the boys through Chapel Lane. About 100 orphans also attended the school. By the early twentieth century the school was still in use, but extensive renovations were required, only made possible through fund-raising efforts.[43] One such was the Calaroga Fête, which was opened by the lord mayor and lady mayoress on 17 April 1911. In his opening remarks, the mayor said:

> It was absolutely necessary in this age of competition that every child should receive such a measure of education as would enable it to earn a livelihood in honour and decency. The future greatness of Dublin depended largely upon Dublin itself. They must have a great force of educated opinion to bring Dublin back into the front of the world, where, long ago, it had been a leading light.[44]

The other school on Little Denmark Street was situated at No. 27. It faced the opening onto Rotunda Market on the opposite side of the street. A plaque informed the passer-by that it was 'St Mary's parochial school, erected 1753, repaired 1847'.[45] By the early part of the twentieth century, the building, still known locally as the Protestant Home, had become a residential property, with voting registers for the period listing up to eighteen inhabitants. One of the most famous was Irish actor Harry Glenville (d. 1910), who toured with Edmund Faulkner and had hits with plays such as *Eileen Oge*. His three sons, Shaun, Matthew and Herbert, also went on to have careers in the theatrical world.

Another interesting building in this part of the market was No. 28 Little Denmark Street. Set back from the pavement, a plaque bore the following inscription:

'This Charity House was built and endowed in the year 1755 by Tristram Fortick, a citizen of Dublin, late of Fortick's Grove in the Co. of Dublin, Esq; for the use of reduced women who had lived in good repute.'[46]

Tristram Fortick, the philanthropist who lived in Fortick's Grove, endowed his almshouse with the rents and profits accruing from several houses he built on Jervis Street. The layout of the almshouse resembled that of Damer's charity house on Great Britain Street, albeit on a smaller scale. It had a brick front, but the rear was constructed from rusticated stone. The street in front had a water cock and pipe, with a yard and grass plot to the rear. Fortick's original scheme of dividing the house into thirty-two apartments proved overly ambitious, however. Half were later allotted as coal holes and each widow was allowed one for her personal use.[47] By the early twentieth century it had fallen into a dangerous state of repair.[48]

Another building associated with Fortick's estate was No. 29 Little Denmark Street – a four-storey house with a shop at ground-floor level. A private entrance stood to the right of the shopfront. In 1914 it was the subject of a fierce legal battle fought over non-payment of rent. During the course of the ensuing court case, one of the barristers underscored the street's long history when he noted with some exasperation that it was one of the most complicated cases with which he had ever had to deal. The statement of title alone would take the better part of two days – there being 'a string of documents on both sides from 1705 down to recent times'.[49]

Towards the Henry Street end of Little Denmark Street stood two further land-mark buildings. The first of these (No. 33) housed the 'Amicable Benefit Society'.[50] During the late nineteenth century it was turned over to the Typographical Provident Society – a militant printers' union that took active steps to prevent the use of strike breakers, more commonly referred to as 'black-leg labour' in trade disputes.[51] The other was Denmark House (No. 39) on the Henry Street corner. This four-storey red-brick building was built during the early twentieth century. It housed the Irish Gown Manufacturers (known locally as 'The Gowns'). Among other things, the Gowns manufactured blouses and mantles. The directors were B. Reynolds and H. Masoff. On 7 November 1957 the Irish Fashion Company made a home there, having trans-ferred from Middle Abbey Street.[52] A decade later the Irish Button Company oper-ated a sophisticated injection-moulding operation from the same premises.[53]

On 1 January 1926, 2RN (later Raidió Éireann) made its inaugural broadcast from a little room above the employment exchange at No. 36 Little Denmark Street. Douglas Hyde, founder of the Gaelic League and first president of Ireland, made a speech, first in English 'for any strangers who may be listening in' and then in Irish. Among those present was the station's first director, Seamus Clandillon, who was noted for his enthusiasm for the new station. When he was short-handed, he was said to press-gang strollers on Denmark Street into performing broadcasts, and his wife Mairead Ní Annagain was such a regular contributor that listeners nicknamed her 'Mairead Ní On-Again'. In the early days, the station broadcast for just three hours, beginning at 7.30 p.m. with a tuning note to help listeners adjust their receivers.[54] The station moved to the GPO in 1928.

Market Street (The Lime Yard/Fountain Lane or Row)

This thoroughfare is mentioned in various trade directories from the 1840s onwards. It ran from Riddall's Row to Moore Place. Visible on the Ordnance Survey map of 1866 is a public fountain, which may explain why it was sometimes called 'Fountain Lane' or 'Row'.[55] An alternative name, 'The Lime Yard', referred to the practice of washing its walls with lime to deaden the smell of manure and blood from slaughtered animals.

In 1879 the North Dublin Poor Law Union identified the Lime Yard as an ideal site for a corporation abattoir. What recommended it was its central location in the market area, which obviated the need for additional assistants, horses and carts.[56] By the 1940s a number of slaughterhouses were still in operation there in a row of small, whitewashed cottages. These lay behind the butchers' shops on Moore Street.

On 21 June 1970 the *Sunday Independent* reported that an escaping heifer scattered pedestrians as it raced from the Lime Yard to Parnell Street – an occasional hazard of market life.

Mason's Market (Row)

This short thoroughfare of eight houses ran from Cole's Lane to Horseman's Row. According to Griffith's Valuation, each was owned by Patrick Fitzpatrick. During

A man and children watch the butcher at work in The Lime Yard. *(Courtesy of RTÉ Stills Library)*

the mid nineteenth century it was home to a cooper and clothes-mangler. *The Freeman's Journal* of 20 July 1892 outlines a further mix of shops, including grocers, second-hand clothes markets, furniture shops and shoe shops. Mason's Market was also home to a dairy and coal shop, a carpenter and a cabinet-maker. Some of these businesses were still in operation in the early twentieth century.

McCann's Lane

This meandering little lane was a continuation of Sampson's Lane on the opposite side of Cole's Lane. It was named after Michael McCann, who owned property there, as well as on Little Denmark Street. Various memorials of indenture confuse or conflate the street with Cole's Lane, but maps from the mid nineteenth century show that it was quite separate. The proprietors of some of the shops on Henry Street (which backed onto the lane) used it for stables or auction rooms.[57] During the 1920s and 1930s much of the site was cleared, and Charles E. Goad's insurance map of 1957 depicts it as a straight thoroughfare.[58]

The J&G Campbell Tea Company was established on Moore Lane in 1797. *(Author's collection)*

Moore Lane (Old Brickfield Lane)

This thoroughfare appears on John Rocque's map of 1756 as 'Old Brickfield Lane'. It was renamed Moore Lane in 1773.[59] Still in existence today, it runs from Parnell Street (Great Britain Street) to Henry Place (Off Lane). It effectively marked the edge of the boundary between the parishes of St Mary and St Thomas.

Moore Lane, 1952.
(Courtesy of the Military Archives)

By the mid nineteenth century it was home to the offices of a number of government appointees. These included a Dublin Metropolitan Police solicitor, the Marshal of the High Court of Admiralty and the Deputy Sergeant at Arms. Businesses there included Storey's public house, the Atlas Engine House and a number of livery stables. C. Penney operated a chemical works on the lane, and there was also a lodging house nearby.

During the 1890s the lane was home to the offices of *The Freeman's Journal*. Local children nicknamed it 'Marble Lane'. They used to forage for the glass marbles used as stoppers in the necks of bottles made by a local mineral-water firm.[60] In 1916 the rebels who fled from the GPO used some crates from this factory to form a temporary barricade. Moore Lane was also the site of Ireland's first Tayto Crisps factory, established by Joseph Murphy in 1954.

Moore Street Market

The entrance to this narrow shopping street was gained through an archway with a nineteenth-century red-brick plaque that bore its name. It ran from Moore Street to Market Street and was similar in layout to Cole's Lane, paved with large granite flags along its length. During the nineteenth century it was dominated by butchers' stalls. John and William Hogan had a large butcher shop at No. 5, which supplied meat, including venison, to His Excellency the Earl of Bessborough. A century later, it was home to clothes sellers. In his novel, *Young Man with a Dream*, Kenneth Sheils Reddin describes how the market appeared to him during the 1940s: 'As they turned aside and passed through the archway into Moore Market, among the little clothes shops with their jockey cap eaves meeting like bushy eyebrows across the narrow channels, the clamour melted away and they were left at peace.'[61]

Moore Place (Limekiln Lane)

The entrance to this cobblestone street was gained via an archway that led west from Moore Street towards Cole's Lane. From the mid nineteenth century it comprised a close-packed network of slaughterhouses, lairs and stables. A large wooden butt took pride of place in the centre of the street and was used by the slaughterhouse hen for washing their hands. Sean O'Casey recalls that they were 'big bullock men greasy with the fat of dying and dead animals; kind under it all … gave all they could of the bloody issues into the clutching hands of the tattered poor'.[62] The alternative title for this street, Limekiln Lane, refers to an adjacent yard owned by William Pearse, where lime for whitewashing, plastering and brick-bonding was burned.

Moore Street

Moore Street still runs in a straight, unbroken line from Parnell Street to Henry Street. It has existed since 1728, when it was known as 'Moor' Street.[63] It was named after its principal landowner, Henry Moore, the 1st Earl of Drogheda, who also bequeathed his name to Henry Street, North Earl Street, Off Lane (probably) and Drogheda Street (later Sackville Street, now O'Connell Street).

Essentially, the street was constructed in two stages. By the early eighteenth century it was still largely incomplete on its eastern side. John Rocque's map of 1756 shows a large plot of vacant ground extending towards Sackville Street called the 'Old Brick Field'. This probably refers to a clayey area of ground where the bricks used to build the adjacent Drogheda Street were baked. Towards the Henry Street end vacant plots were laid out in long strips with modest houses built on them.

Nos 10–25 (which housed the final headquarters of the 1916 leadership) were built in a terrace around 1763 – the second phase of construction. Some of the houses such as those at Nos 19 and 20, had well-laid-out, ornate gardens to their rear.[64]

At this point in its history, Moore Street was a quiet, residential part of the city inhabited by sedan-chair-makers, coachbuilders and stuccodores such as Robert West (d. 1790). No. 41 was a private nursing home run by Dr William Collum of the nearby Rotunda Hospital. His lack of attendance at the Rotunda brought him into conflict with the hospital governors.[65] Other noted residents were London-born actor Thomas Wilks (1746–1812), who lived on the street in 1805, and the writer William Carleton (1794–1869), who lived there in 1818.[66] That same year, a hospital opened at No. 20 for the treatment of skin diseases, known as the Dublin Infirmary of Cutaneous Disorders. It was operated as a private concern by Dr William Wallace, a surgeon at Jervis Street Infirmary, who, in 1833, published a treatise on venereal disease and its varieties. The premises closed after his death in 1837.

By the date of John Rocque's map (1756), Moore Street had two intersecting thoroughfares – Gregg Street and Bunting Lane.

It was only during the latter part of the nineteenth century that the street became known for its grocers, butchers, poulterers and victuallers. This transition is evident in *Thom's Directory* for 1842. Whereas one half of the street (from No. 30 onwards) was dominated by fishmongers, grocers and cheese sellers, the other half was home to a dazzling array of businesses. These included tinplate workers, a chandler, a mattress-maker, an attorney, a cork manufacturer, at least two hairdressing concerns, a tailor, an architect, a slater and a builder. At No. 18, Thomas Champion ran a cabinet-making business, but also imported leeches. No. 19 was home to the china and glass showrooms of Frederick Vodrey (1845–97), whose pottery factory to the rear turned out ornamental vases with colourful glazes. Emily Macklin had a French and English School at No. 28.

Above: **Carmel Mooney at her stall.** *(Courtesy of Darren Kinsella)*

Opposite: **Martin & Son, No. 55 Moore Street.** *Left to right:* **Joe Eglington, Bobby Bates, Mickey Ramsey, Jimmy Martin. The street once boasted around twenty butchers' shops.** *(Courtesy of Eamon Martin)*

In an era before food cooperatives appeared on the street, such businesses jostled for space with shops such as Michael Kearney's 'Great Provision and Italian Warehouse', which boasted a range of items catering for the 'respectable class'. Such a variety of enterprises would be more at home on a town high street today, reflecting the fact that Dublin was once a much smaller city.

By the middle of the nineteenth century, the handmade yellow bricks with which many of the houses on Moore Street were built had begun to crumble, and the façades were replaced with machine-made red Victorian brick. This process, evident in other parts of the city, can still be seen on the eastern side of the street, where the line of the original apex roofs is just visible behind the flat parapets. Further damage to the street resulted from shell and bullet bombardment during the 1916 Rising, when many of the buildings at the Henry Street end were destroyed by fire. Afterwards, Nos 1–7 were completely rebuilt in red brick with limestone dressing.

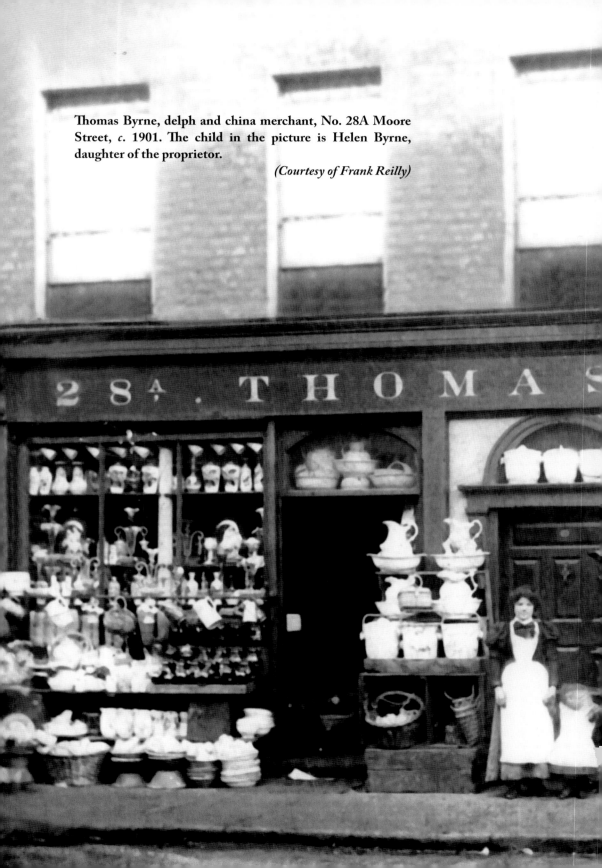

Thomas Byrne, delph and china merchant, No. 28A Moore Street, *c.* 1901. The child in the picture is Helen Byrne, daughter of the proprietor.

(Courtesy of Frank Reilly)

This entrance to Mulligan's Court near the Henry Street end of Moore Street is now used for storing goods.

(Author's collection)

Mulligan's Court (Melville Lane)

This long-forgotten lane is shown on a series of Ordnance Survey maps from 1846. Running north to south from Off Lane (Henry Place), it joined Clarke's Court leading into Moore Street. It was named after Edward Mulligan, who owned property there from 1805 onwards. One of Mulligan's most notable purchases was in 1810, when he acquired a parcel of property from George Daniel, a captain in the Enniskillen Regiment. In doing so, he changed the name of the alley from its earlier title of Melville Lane.[67] In 1862 all of this property, including several houses in Henry Street, Off Lane and Clarke's Court passed, via the Landed Estate's Court, from Mulligan's widow Julia to a number of private speculators from Liverpool.[68] By the mid nineteenth century the buildings had degenerated into tenements. In the late 1870s the Off Lane entrance was closed up and it became a blind alley.

Murray's Court

Approached from the Henry Street direction, this little court was situated off Moore Lane, prior to where it met the junction of Sackville Lane. The houses, which backed onto Nos 21 and 23 Moore Street, are marked clearly on the 1866 Ordnance Survey map.[69] It was named after Cornelius Murray, who, in January 1881, was fined 20s for its unsanitary condition.[70]

Norfolk Market

This little thoroughfare ran from Great Britain Street to Riddall's Row and was named after a bust of the Duke of Norfolk which stood at one end.[71] There were twenty-four properties in the market, but by the mid nineteenth century most lay empty. Painter Fergus O'Ryan's depiction of the market from the 1930s shows that, as in nearby Cole's Lane, traders here sold clothes. The market comprised a number of close-packed shops or stalls protected by awnings. A gas lamp, slung from the crossbeam of an arch at the Great Britain Street end, shed light on what must, at times, have been a gloomy place. An iron hand pump with a lion's head in the middle of the lane provided the sole water supply for the inhabitants. By the mid twentieth century, some of the older houses at the Riddall's Row end had been demolished, making way for a number of corrugated iron structures.

One of the lane's most noted residents was John Moloney, secretary of the Amalgamated Society of Tailors (Emerald Branch) and member of the Dublin Trades Council, who lived at No. 10.[72]

Off Lane Yard

During the mid nineteenth century, this yard was home to John Cullen's dairy.

Parnell Street (Great Britain Street)

Great Britain Street was originally laid out in the first half of the eighteenth-century. It was much narrower than today's thoroughfare, which was renamed Parnell Street in October 1911 to coincide with the unveiling of a monument to the 'Uncrowned King', Charles Stewart Parnell, by John Dillon, MP.

The street, which consisted 'mainly of small shops with three and four-storey houses above' was constructed in the distinctive Dutch 'Billie' style with elegant curvilinear façades.[73] Nos 157 and 158, among the last to be erected in the city (*c.* 1740), are still in existence, albeit with high, flattened parapets.

The *Dublin Directory* of 1778 lists a 'cart and waggon maker' at No. 73, as well as two upholsters at Nos 31 and 163. These were probably subcontracted to neighbouring coach-building firms. During a later period, one of the street's most famous residents was Young Irelander James Fintan Lalor (1807–49), who lived at No. 39. One of the most significant buildings on the western end of the street was

Corner of the old Williams & Woods factory on King's Inn Street.

(Author's collection)

230

Simpson's Hospital (No. 204). Founded by George Simpson, a wealthy merchant from Jervis Street, it was built in 1787 as an asylum for 'blind and gouty men in reduced circumstances'.[74] Simpson, who suffered from the latter ailment himself, is said to have been inspired to bequeath a portion of his estate to founding the hospital. After he and his wife died, thirteen trustees were assigned to carry out his wishes. Soon, the sight of the old men in their blue pilot-cloth coats and tall black felt hats became a familiar one on the street.

At the time of the 1916 Rising, the building was home to Williams & Woods Ltd, the renowned preserves and sweets manufacturers. Scores of schoolchildren used to follow the trucks as they entered the premises, using the little knives they carried for sharpening pencils to cut the jute bags and rob apples.

The local girls who worked at the factory packed beetroot and soups and learned how to make up the ingredients. Many dreaded working in the jam section because the conditions there were very difficult. The jam workers were always wet as a result of the fruit pulping and wore clogs and rubber aprons to try to keep dry. During the strawberry season they got overtime on a Saturday and additional girls were taken on. In good weather they could be seen sitting outside removing green stalks from the strawberries.

Across the road from Williams & Woods, almost on the corner of Little Denmark Street, was a substantial three-storey over-basement building. This was Joseph Damer's Charity House (No. 27). In an indenture drawn up in 1716, Damer stipulated that the house was to provide for the maintenance and support of poor widows. He lived an extraordinarily long life, dying at the age of ninety-one in 1718.[75]

From the outset, the charity house cared for children as well as for widows, and a separate school was later established. The

Exterior of Williams & Woods, Parnell Street, previously the Simpson's Hospital building.
(Courtesy of Peter Pearson)

231

The original Peat's store on the corner of Chapel Lane and Parnell Street opened in 1934. It sold radiograms and wet cell batteries, as well as prams, bicycles and other goods. (*Courtesy of Dublin City Library and Archive*)

terms of admission were exacting. In order to qualify for a room, a widow had to be Protestant and living in demonstrably poor circumstances. Few of the local street traders qualified and the governors adopted a particularly stringent attitude towards the Roman Catholic Church. Widow Mary Irwin, for instance, 'had a priest at the time of her sickness, Contrary to the Rules of the House – by directions at the request of the Rev. Mr. Purdon and Dr Cuthbert, it was stated such visits were only hastening dissolution'.[76] Most inhabitants were the widows of government clerks or those involved in higher-end businesses such as coach-making. Each was given a room with an allowance of bread, light and fuel. Drunkenness and other anti-social behaviours were frowned upon, but the women were allowed to keep pigs and fowl.

By the early nineteenth century, the house had fallen on hard times, as explained in Wharburton, Whitelaw and Walsh's *History of Dublin*:

Instead of that cheerful neatness and cleanliness so grateful to the eye of the spectator in the habitations of the poor, it is here disgusted with walls

Mick's Bar, No. 49 Parnell Street. This 200-year-old pub had another entrance onto the adjacent Horseman's Row. It was said to have been frequented by Michael Collins during the War of Independence. It continued in business for some years after the top two storeys collapsed.
(*Courtesy of Dublin City Library and Archive*)

embroidered with dirt and smoke, windows from filth scarce pervious to the light, and by a ruinous ceiling, threatening destruction to the inhabitants, of which some fragments have already fallen. The roof has lately been repaired, but the timber work of the building not having been painted, as we were informed, since 1797, is rapidly hastening to decay; and we must add, that the window which originally lighted the lower gallery having been accidentally broken, has been injudiciously built up, so that the wretched inhabitants of this floor are necessitated to grope their way to their apartments through darkness visible.[77]

Despite these difficulties, the charity continued to operate well into the twentieth century.

Where Parnell Street meets O'Connell Street, one of the main buildings of note is the Rotunda Hospital. The foundation of this Dublin landmark may be traced back to 1748, when Bartholomew Mosse acquired a lease of four acres and one

The rather gloomy exterior of the Damer Institute – home to Protestant widows and children from 1724 until shortly before the construction of the ILAC Centre.
(Courtesy of the Irish Architectural Archive)

rood plantation measure from William Naper on the north side of the street. The first stone was laid in 1751, the adjoining grounds becoming known as the new gardens and bowling green – later Rutland (Parnell) Square.[78] William Corbett, whose business was at No. 57 Great Britain Street, bought the copyright for *Wilson's Dublin Directory* in 1802, the first of its kind in the city.

By the late nineteenth century, tram lines had been laid on Parnell Street, adding a new sense of bustle and industry. Along Great Britain Street clanked the cumbersome swaying tramcars. Seamus Scully recalled 'their jerking trolleys spluttering coloured sparks from the overhead shiny steel wires, and their iron wheels thudding and grinding over the shrieking iron rails.'[79]

During the 1970s and 1980s the street was widened as part of the plan for the city's inner tangent relief road. Thereafter it languished as an open, somewhat toothless-looking eyesore until the mid 1990s, when most of the south side was reconstructed. These new buildings may lack intrinsic value, but at the very least they have restored some sense of commercial vitality to the street.

Perry's Court

This court was named after John Perry. It was located just off Cole's Lane, near the Henry Street junction.[80] Today, the site is occupied by the Dunne's Stores building. It is shown on the Ordnance Survey map of 1847, but does not appear on subsequent maps of the area.[81] *Thom's Directory* for 1850 describes two houses in tenements there, but it seems that the court was completely built over not long afterwards.

Riddall's Row (Gregg Street)

This street, which appears on John Rocque's map of 1756 and in Walter Harris' *History and Antiquities of the City of Dublin* (1766), was part of the old 'Bull Park'.[82] It was originally known as Gregg Street or Gregg Lane – a long thoroughfare that may well have been in existence since the mid seventeenth century. It extended towards Gloucester (Sean MacDermott) Street until the construction of Drogheda Street during the 1750s divided it in half, the eastern end eventually becoming Cathal Brugha Street.

During the early nineteenth century it was renamed after a local weaver named James Riddall (d. 1832). The Duke of Richmond was so impressed with his racquet court that he had him awarded with a knighthood. Thereafter he served as City Sheriff from 1809 to 1810 and City Sword Bearer from 1817 to 1831.[83] Riddall married the daughter of a man named Speer from Moore Street in 1796. As part of the settlement, a number of Speer's local properties were vested in Riddall's trustees and heirs, the former reserving power to make leases on certain terms.[84]

By the middle of the nineteenth century, Riddall's Row was dominated by meat butchers. A total of twenty-four are listed in *Thom's Directory* for 1842. By 1901 most of these had moved out, replaced in their turn by a mix of shoe, clothes and furniture dealers. One of the longest-surviving families on the row was that of Keogh, whose descendants were still running a second-hand shoe business there in the 1960s.

Rotunda Market (Cash Lane or Row)

This butchers' market began trading in the late eighteenth century and was named after the nearby hospital of the same name. It was described in 1807 by Richard Cumberland as the greatest market in Dublin, but he also criticised the narrowness of its passages.[85]

From the early nineteenth century, Rotunda Market also went by the name of 'Cash Row', named after city alderman John Cash (1759–1833), who lived at No. 34 Rutland (Parnell) Square. Cash, who was a stationer by trade, served a term as lord mayor from 1813 to 1814 and helped to form the Hibernian Church

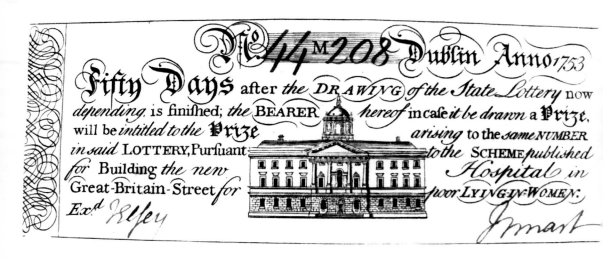

Missionary Society.[86] He was also a director of the Dublin Fishery Company and a committee member of the Mendicity Institution. In Griffith's Valuation, all twenty-four properties on the lane were recorded as belonging to him.[87]

After his death, the houses passed to his son – also named John. In 1839 he came to court over a refusal to pay for meat given to him by a Cole's Lane butcher. In his defence Cash claimed that the meat had been accepted in lieu of a large rental debt.[88]

By the late 1890s the lane comprised a cluster of second-hand shops with upstairs tenement accommodation. One of the principal landowners was Elias Eliassoff from Little Denmark Street.[89] By the 1920s some portions of the street had become waste ground and it was targeted for demolition by Dublin Corporation.

Sackville Court

This cluster of houses was situated off Sackville Lane. During the 1840s it was home to stuccodore Edward H. Quinn.

Sackville Lane (now O'Rahilly Parade)

This lane, which leads onto Moore Lane from Moore Street, appears on a series of nineteenth-century Ordnance Survey maps. Many of the buildings had extensive stores and vaults, with *Thom's Directory* for 1842 listing a shoemaker, provision dealer, carpenter, paper stainer and rag-and-bone dealer. Today it is best known for its memorial to The O'Rahilly, devised by Dublin-based artist Shane Cullen. It carries the following verse written by William Butler Yeats:

> What remains to sing about
> But of the death he met
> Stretched under a doorway
> Somewhere off Henry Street;

Left: Lottery tickets like this helped to construct the Rotunda Hospital. The scheme was insti-gated by the founder of the hospital, Bartholomew Mosse, in 1751. The prize office was located in the old Philharmonic Room in Fishamble Street. *(F.S. Bourke Collection, Ms. 10,707, courtesy of the National Library of Ireland)*

This evocative image, taken *c.* 1900, gives a sense
of how close-packed Dublin's own *souk* once was.
*(Reproduced by permission of the Royal Society of
Antiquaries of Ireland)*

They that found him found upon
The door above his head
'Here died The O'Rahilly
RIP.' writ in blood.
How goes the weather?[90]

Sampson's Lane (Birchin Lane/Bunting Lane)

The entrance to this thoroughfare may still be found near the Henry Street end of Moore Street. It originally appeared in *The History and Antiquities of Dublin* (1766) as Birchin Lane. By about 1780 it had changed its name to 'Sampson's Lane', an association perhaps with George Simpson's sugar house on Cole's Lane. Of note, however, a merchant named Michael Sampson also owned land there in the early part of the eighteenth century.[91]

During a later period Sampson's Lane housed a school for Protestant children. On 2 August 1819 it was the scene of a local dispute 'when a Popish priest entered, interrupted the business … and forced the children out'.[92]

By the early 1900s the lane was dominated by slaughterhouses which dealt in sheep, cattle and other livestock. The well-known name Olhaussen appears in connection with one of these.[93] There were several haylofts and fodder stores, and some businesses kept lock-up facilities there. During the evacuation of the GPO, a party of men hid in a factory owned by Williams & Woods at No. 13.

Further development was carried out in 1913, with two completely new two-storey houses (Nos 1 and 2) built on the northern side of the lane near the corner of Moore Street.[94]

On its southern side, a small row of late-nineteenth-century, two-storey artisan dwellings, with rusticated granite window lintels, remain.

Taaffe's Row (Smith Alley)

Smith Alley, an alternative name for this thoroughfare, may reflect the type of work that was once carried out there. In the early nineteenth century it was renamed after a rather gregarious poulterer named Richard Taaffe. In April 1830 he had a row with a fellow tradesman from Castle Market about the sale of some pigeons and daws, and the men prepared to fight a duel. When a peace officer was despatched to speak to Taaffe, he found him preparing a turkey for sale. A knife, a sword and a pair of old holster pistols lay alongside, together with the following rather macabre document:

> I, Richard Taaffe, of Cole's Lane market, in the city of Dublin, chicken butcher, being of sound and disposing mind, and strong in body, do hereby constitute this my last will and testament … I bequeath my soul to God, my body to the Resurrectionists, medical students and scalping knives.[95]

In later years, Taaffe's Row was home to two carpenters, a coach trimmer and a broker who doubled up as a Japanner – a man skilled in the art of lacquerwork in the Japanese style. A public fountain provided water for the residents. During the same period there was a small court or yard behind the street with a dung-caked fountain in the middle named 'Taaffe's Market'. The houses were built back to back without yards. Four outside water closets were located on the street for the convenience of the residents.

In 1899 a case was brought against a descendant of Taaffe due to the state of ten of the houses on the row. Describing the living conditions that he found over a series of disused ground-floor shops, Dr Charles Cameron testified in court that 'the ascents to the stories [sic] are made through very narrow and defective stairs' and when these were momentarily lit up by the opening of the door of one of the wretched apartments within, he had 'ready and conclusive reason to appreciate the want of a proper circulation of fresh air'.[96]

Several of the houses were removed, with apertures opened in the remaining buildings to assist ventilation. By 1926 all of the houses on the southern side of the street had disappeared, replaced by a high wall that marked the boundary of the 'Rag, Bone and Metal Stores'.[97]

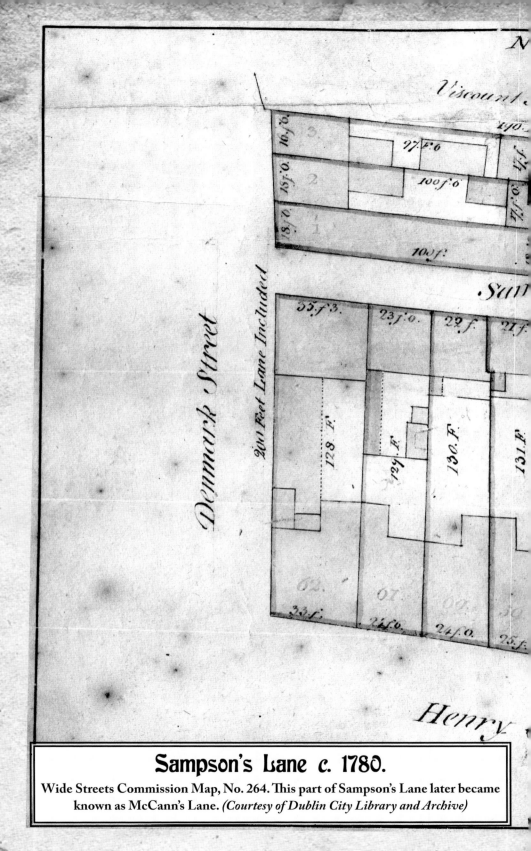

Sampson's Lane c. 1780.

Wide Streets Commission Map, No. 264. This part of Sampson's Lane later became known as McCann's Lane. *(Courtesy of Dublin City Library and Archive)*

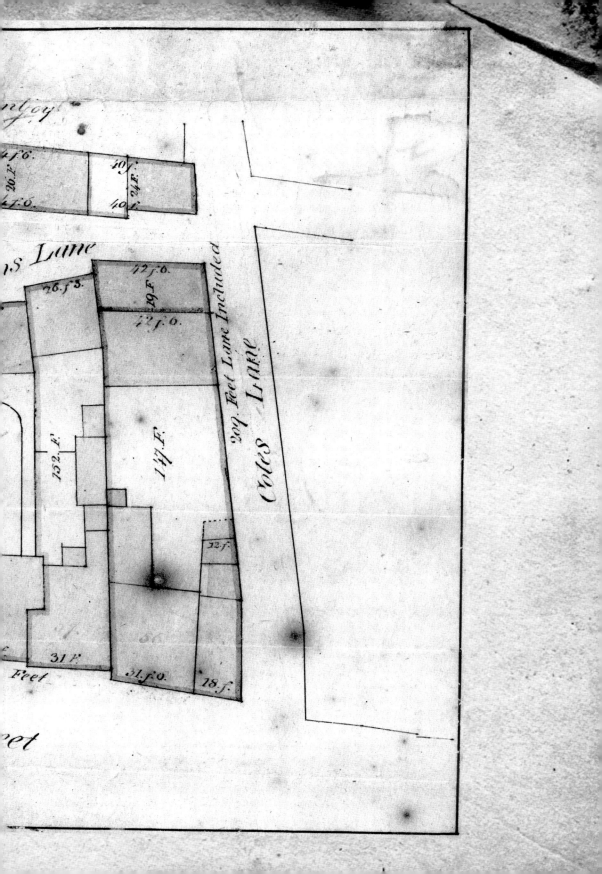

...nfoy

26 f. 6.

40 f.

24 F.

40 f.

...s Lane

26 f. 3.

12 f. 6.

19 F.

12 f. 0.

152 F.

147 F.

209 Feet Lane Included

Coles Lane

12 f.

31 F.

Feet

31 f. 0.

18 f.

Conclusion

It is difficult to sum up the story of any market – least of all Moore Street, which has existed in one form or another for over two centuries. However, some of this history is recorded in local ballads. In 'Dublin Jack of All Trades', written during the early 1800s, we are told that our hero was 'in Cole's Lane, a jobbing butcher', but, by the time the mournful Butcher Boy appeared in broadsheets towards the end of the century, this trade had moved east into Moore Street. As the market continues to adapt, it may well achieve fame in the near future for some other kind of industry – perhaps even giving rise to a new ballad or two.

In the face of such changes, Moore Street's humour or 'citrus wit' (as Brendan O'Carroll calls it) has always been its one constant. During the 1870s the local characters included greengrocer Darby Blake and his fellow traders, one of whom pleaded of a plump customer: 'Say you'll buy your meat from me, and I'll make my fortune!' During the 1940s that observational comedy was still there. When asked whether her tomatoes were Irish, one trader replied, 'God save us. Tomatoes only five pence a pound and she wants to know their nationality!'

Not surprisingly, the area has attracted its fair share of writers, artists and poets. Donal Lunny and Brian Bolger's 'Emmet Folk' and 'Parnell Folk' used to play gigs in local pubs such as Maher's, and Patrick Kavanagh could often be found drinking in Paddy Madigan's. When challenged over a pint to define a Dublin man, the bard famously replied, 'A Dublin man doesn't go home for his holidays.'

At the same time, much of Moore Street's characteristic wit was born out of resilience in the face of grinding poverty. Irish trade-union leader Jim Larkin spoke about how he had seen ragged street children crawling under the barrows of stallholders in search of rotten fruit, and local historian Seamus Scully winced to hear him describe its alleys and lanes as one of the worst slums in Dublin.

So much of what has been written about Moore Street over the past fifty years has been retrospective. Newspaper pieces and articles have tended to commemorate rather than celebrate what remains of it, committing it to record; foreshadowing its demise. One might be forgiven, therefore, for failing to realise that there is still a living market there. Yet, despite all the odds, it has clung on, adapting to changing circumstances amid an influx of foreign nationalities – those same people who single-handedly reversed a steep inner city population decline for the first time in decades, bringing with them a demand for new, more cosmopolitan foodstuffs. 'Go down to Moore Street and get your nose educated,' Jimmy O'Dea once said. Today this dictum is more likely to apply to the smell of Middle Eastern spices or the aroma of French bread, but, in a sense, the market has always been an international space. Even before the First World War, Egyptian onions were sold there and one often forgets the distance over which fruits such as the humble banana had to travel; the market is a place where worlds converge.

For all its vibrancy and colour, however, Moore Street is nothing without its people. From the stoic flowerseller, who can still be heard telling her jostling customers that 'patience is a virtue', to the fishmonger guarding her produce from the craw of an expectant seagull, the traders are the very essence of the market. Without them the cobbles mean very little. They are the real living heritage of Moore Street – the 'heart of the rowl' – whose way of life is worth saving before it is too late.

Notes

Abbreviations

GL   Gilbert Library (Dublin)
IADT Institute of Art, Design and Technology
NAI   National Archives of Ireland
NLI   National Library of Ireland
ROD   Registry of Deeds, Dublin
TCML Trinity College Map Library, Dublin
RSAI Royal Society of Antiquaries of Ireland

Part 1: The Story of the Market

1. *Dublin Monthly Magazine, Being a New Series of the Citizen and Including the Native Music of Ireland*, vol. I, January–June 1842, p. 267.
2. John Warburton, James Whitelaw and Robert Walsh, *History of the City of Dublin: From the Earliest Accounts to the Present Time*, vol. II (Dublin, 1818), p. 1129.
3. Meeting of the Corporation for Paving the Streets of Dublin (Dublin, 1781) p. 4.
4. *Calendar of Ancient Records of Dublin*, vol. XIV, ed. Lady Gilbert (Dublin, 1909), p. 91.
5. *The Irish Times*, 7 August 1873.
6. *The Freeman's Journal*, 11 July 1878.
7. Report to Chief Secretary (NAI CSORP 1884/7540).
8. *The Freeman's Journal*, 11 March 1840.
9. Byelaws with Respect to Slaughterhouses, 1879 (GL, Corporation Reports &c).
10. Minute Book of Directors of the Watch, 1750–70 (NAI P 4960–1).
11. *The Freeman's Journal*, 24 October 1840.
12. *Weekly News*, 7 December 1867.
13. *Bananas on a Breadboard: Stories from the Market Area, Dublin* (Dublin, 2009) (video).
14. *Bananas on a Breadboard*.
15. James Whitelaw, *An Account of the Enumeration of the Inhabitants of the City of Dublin* (Dublin, 1805).
16. UCD School of Architecture, *Moore Street – A Report* (Dublin, 1974), p. 6.
17. *The Dublin Builder*, 15 March 1861, p. 456.
18. Jacinta Prunty, *Dublin Slums, 1800–1925: A Study in Urban Geography* (Dublin, 1998), p. 91.
19. Seán O'Casey, *Pictures in the Hallway* (New York, 1942), p. 139.
20. *The Irish Times*, 15 June 1870.
21. Interview with Seamus Marken, 26 November 2011.
22. Interview with Jack Kennerk, 16 June 2011.
23. *The Freeman's Journal*, 18 November 1847.
24. *The Freeman's Journal*, 6 October 1866.
25. *Liverpool Mercury*, 21 October 1875.
26. *The Freeman's Journal*, 1 May 1884.
27. *The Freeman's Journal*, 17 June 1886.
28. *The Irish Times*, 24 February 1920.
29. Interview with Seamus Marken.
30. Tom Geraghty and Trevor Whitehead, *The Dublin Fire Brigade: A History of the Brigade, the Fires and the Emergencies* (Dublin, 2004), p. 115.
31. *Caledonian Mercury*, 20 November 1837.
32. *The Irish Times*, 14 September 1900.
33. *The Irish Times*, 2 January 1915.
34. *The Irish Times*, 4 February 1882.
35. Seán Cronin, *Young Connolly* (Dublin, 1978), p. 34.
36. Conor Cruise O'Brien, 'Passion and Cunning: An Essay on the Politics of W. B. Yeats', in Jonathan Allison (ed.), *Yeats's Political Identities: Selected Essays* (Michigan, 1996), pp. 29–44.
37. Of note, Seán O'Casey describes Captain Brennan in *The Plough and the Stars* as a chicken butcher of the Irish Citizen Army.
38. *Sinn Féin Rebellion Handbook*, compiled by weekly *Irish Times* (Dublin, 1917) and card catalogue of 1916 internees (NAI).
39. *Irish Press*, 16 January 1941.
40. Catherine Tynan, *The Years of the Shadow* (London, 1919), p. 229.

41. Seamus Scully, 'Moore Street – 1916', *Dublin Historical Record*, 39 (2) (1986): 53–63.

42. Insurance assessment for No. 15 Moore Street and Nos 10–12 Moore Street (NAI, Property Losses [Ireland] Committee, 1916, File 297, 3/082/15 and File 118, 3/082/14).

43. Claim of Hannah Price, Nos 11, 22 and 23 Moore Street (NAI, Property Losses [Ireland] Committee, 1916, File 695, 3/082/13).

44. Interview with Seamus O'Rourke, 12 December 2011.

45. Insurance assessment for No. 18 Little Denmark Street (NAI Property Losses [Ireland] Committee, 1916, File 3099, 3/082/43).

46. *Irish Builder*, 16 August 1913.

47. Bill Cullen, *It's a Long Way from Penny Apples* (Cork, 2002), pp. 131–2.

48. Interview with Paddy Ormsby, 16 January 2012. The son of a British Army officer, Paddy's grandfather was born in Peshawar, India. The Gallipoli or Dardanelles Campaign had ended just a few months before the Easter Rising in January 1916.

49. Claim of John F. Alexander, Corporation Market, Dublin (NAI Property Losses [Ireland] Committee, 1916, File 8, 3/082/13).

50. Sketch of Easter Week Operations in the GPO area by Diarmuid Lynch (NLI Ms. 5173).

51. Interview with Maureen Kennerk, granddaughter of Maggie Austin, 1 October 2010.

52. Interview with Christy O'Leary and John Igoe, 23 January 2012.

53. Scully, 'Moore Street – 1916'.

54. Sketch of Easter Week Operations.

55. Claim of Ellen Kelly, Nos 24 and 25 Moore Street (NAI Property Losses [Ireland] Committee, 1916, File 1039, 3/082/23).

56. Interview with Seamus O'Rourke.

57. *Irish Independent*, 6 May 1916.

58. *Ibid.*

59. House of Commons Parliamentary Debate, 1 August 1916, vol. 85, ccl 23–256.

60. Scully, 'Moore Street – 1916'.

61. House of Commons Parliamentary Debate, 1 August 1916, vol. 85, ccl 23–256.

According to the *Sinn Féin Rebellion Handbook*, compiled by weekly *Irish Times* (Dublin, 1917), Mr Dillon was well known in the city for his work for the poor on behalf of the St Vincent de Paul Society.

62. Eamonn Bulfin witness statement (Military Archives, Bureau of Military History, no. 497).

63. Interview with Eamon Martin, 6 January 2012. He further relates that after the rebellion, The O'Rahilly's widow presented a christening robe to Mrs Coyle, Henry's widow, who had been pregnant with their child.

64. Joseph Good witness statement (Military Archives, Bureau of Military History, no. 388).

65. Lorcan Collins and Conor Kostick, *The Easter Rising* (Dublin, 2001).

66. Seán MacEntee, *Episode at Easter* (Dublin and Melbourne, 1966), p. 161.

67. *Ibid.*

68. *The Irish Times*, 4 November 1968.

69. *Catholic Bulletin*, July 1917, p. 459.

70. Joseph Good witness statement.

71. Joseph Good later revealed that an unnamed individual, now clearly identifiable as Mr McKane, made his way to No. 16 where he spoke to one of the leaders (possibly Seán MacDermott). In response to an assurance that if there was 'any carelessness or recklessness … he, MacDermott, would endeavour to bring the culprits before him', McKane stated that he was 'quite satisfied that it was all an accident' (Joseph Good witness statement).

72. James Kavanagh witness statement (Military Archives, Bureau of Military History, no. 889).

73. Eamonn Bulfin witness statement (Military Archives, Bureau of Military History, no. 497).

74. Frank Henderson and Michael Hopkinson (ed.), *Frank Henderson's Easter Rising: Recollections of a Dublin Volunteer* (Cork, 1998), p. 64.

75. James Kavanagh witness statement.

76. Joseph Good witness statement.

77. Charlie McGuire, 'Seán McLoughlin: The Boy Commandant of 1916', *History Ireland*, 14 (2) (2006): 26–30.

78. *Catholic Bulletin*, April 1917, p. 267.

79. Interview with Nurse Elizabeth O'Farrell, *Sunday Independent*, 10 April 1966.

80. The Kelly family who lived nearby were maligned (somewhat unfairly, perhaps, considering the danger) for not responding to The O'Rahilly's calls for a drink of water. In the aftermath of the Rising, this issue would prove to be somewhat contentious amongst the traders on Moore Street.

81. *Catholic Bulletin*, April 1917, pp. 269–70.

82. Victor Sawden Pritchett, *Dublin: A Portrait* (London, 1967), p. 10.

83. Statement by MP Patrick Nugent, House of Commons Parliamentary Debate, 1 August 1916, vol. 85, ccl 23–256.

84. *Irish Builder*, 24 June 1916, p. 288 and 22 July 1916, p. 338.

85. *The Irish Times*, 12 May 1916.

86. Claim of Hannah Price, Nos 11, 22 and 23 Moore Street (NAI Property Losses [Ireland] Committee, 1916, File 695, 3/082/13). There are many similar examples.

87. Insurance assessment for No. 15 Moore Street (NAI Property Losses [Ireland] Committee, 1916, File 297, 3/082/15).

88. Insurance assessment for Nos 14 and 15 Horseman's Row and No. 23 Cole's Lane (NAI Property Losses [Ireland] Committee, 1916, File 114, 3/082/14 and File 201, 3/082/15).

89. Letter from D. M. Kennedy to Chief Commissioner of Police, 23 May 1916, and report of Inspector John Mills, 29 May 1916 (NAI CSORP 9132/1916).

90. *The Irish Times*, 22 July 1916.

91. *Irish Builder*, 10 June 1916.

92. Insurance assessment for Nos 10 and 12 Moore Street, No. 18 Little Denmark Street and No. 16 Moore Street (NAI Property Losses [Ireland] Committee, 1916, File 188, 3/082/14, File 3099, 3/082/43 and File 6965, 3/083/34).

93. Insurance assessment for No. 59 Moore Street (NAI Property Losses [Ireland] Committee, 1916, File 4633, 3/083/11).

94. Report of building contractor Lawrence Whelan regarding Nos 34 and 35 Moore Street (NAI Property Losses [Ireland] Committee, 1916, File 4870, 3/083/13).

95. List of 1916 Rising Internees (NAI CSORP 1918/Carton 5757).

96. Report of Inspector George Love, 9 December 1916 (NAI CSORP 23206/1916).

97. Interview with Seamus Marken.

98. *Irish Press*, 9 September 1939.

99. Interview with Seamus Marken.

100. *Irish Press*, 7 October 1942.

101. *Irish Independent*, 24 February 1945.

102. Interview with Catherine (Kitty) Campion, 23 December 2011.

103. 'Seamus Marken Remembers the Sounds of Moore Street', available online at http://bridge-it.tchpc.tcd.ie/items/show/343 (accessed April 2012).

104. *Irish Press*, 9 July 1945.

105. Interview with Christy O'Leary and John Igoe.

106. Interview with Seamus Marken.

107. *The Irish Times*, 6 January 1943.

108. *The Irish Times*, interview, 15 February 1997.

109. *Irish Press*, 4 December 1945.

110. *Ibid.*

111. Interview with Eamon Martin.

112. Éamonn MacThomáis, *Me Jewel and Darlin' Dublin* (Dublin, 1974), p. 25.

113. Interview with Ken Robinson, 13 May 2011.

114. Interview with Justin Leonard, 18 November 2011.

115. Interview with Bernie Shea, 17 November 2011.

116. Anonymous interviewee.

117. Michael O'Beirne, 'There's No Place Like Moore Street', *The Irish Digest* 73 (2) (1961): 34–5.

118. Interview with Seamus Marken.

119. Extract from 'The Angel' by J. H. Orwell, *The Irish Times*, 6 April 1946.

120. Interview with Martin (Willie) Higgins, 21 December 2011.

121. Seamus Scully, 'Ghosts of Moore Street', *Dublin Historical Record*, 25 (2) (1972): 54–63.

122. Interview with Eamon Martin.

123. Interview with Garrett Keogh, 21 January 2012.

124. *Ibid.*

125. Dominic Behan, *Teems of Times and Happy Returns* (Dublin, 1979), p. 131.

126. Michael O'Beirne, *And the Moon at Night: A Dubliner's Story* (Belfast, 1981), p. 28.

127. *Irish Press*, 16 January 1941. 'The Nile Side' referred to the north face of the pil-

lar which recorded Nelson's 1798 victory in Egypt. Selling on that side would have afforded the sellers some protection from the biting Liffey winds. The three other faces of the pillar recorded victories at Cape St Vincent (1797), Copenhagen (1801) and Trafalgar (1805).

128. Interview with Bernie Shea.
129. *Ibid.*
130. Cullen, *It's a Long Way from Penny Apples*, p. 179.
131. Interview with Bill Cullen, 18 May 2011.
132. *Protestant Penny Magazine, a Collection of Original Essays and Anecdotes* (Dublin, 1836), p. 118.
133. *Dublin Warder*, 18 July 1835.
134. Interview with Seamus Marken.
135. *The Irish Builder*, 1 December 1881, p. 354.
136. *The Irish Times*, 31 March 1860.
137. *The Dublin Builder*, 1 December 1860, p. 374.
138. *The Freeman's Journal*, 20 January 1886.
139. *Irish Builder*, 15 March 1888, pp. 79–80.
140. UCD, *Moore Street – A Report*, p. 12.
141. *The Irish Times*, 13 November 1940.
142. *Ibid.*
143. UCD, *Moore Street – A Report*, p. 12.
144. Interview with Garrett Keogh.
145. *The Irish Times*, 18 February 1956.
146. Charles Abrams, *Urban Renewal Project in Ireland – Dublin* (Dublin and New York, 1961), p. 105.
147. Cullen, *It's a Long Way from Penny Apples*, p. 138.
148. *Build* magazine, quoted by Frank McDonald in *The Destruction of Dublin* (Dublin, 1985), p. 151.
149. UCD, *Moore Street – A Report*, p. 16.
150. *The Irish Times*, 26 September 1968.
151. *The Irish Times*, 13 August 1974.
152. *The Irish Times*, 4 October 1968.
153. *The Irish Times*, 11 October 1968.
154. *Sunday Independent*, 7 January 1968.
155. McDonald, *The Destruction of Dublin*, p. 163.
156. Interview with Garrett Keogh.
157. *Irish Independent*, 31 July 2004.
158. Interview with Salim Ullah Khan, 10 December 2011.
159. See *Moore Street Masala*, 4 August 2009, available online at http://www.screenscene.ie/index.php?/grade_and_telecine/moore_street_masala (accessed 16 April 2012).
160. John Walters, *Business as Usual* (IADT, National Film School, Dublin 2010).
161. Interview with Keith Duffy, 8 March 2012.
162. Interview with Patrick Cooney, 29 January 2012.

Part 3: Streets of the Market Area

1. Probate of the Last Will and Testament of John French Senior, 11 November 1881 (in private possession of Marie and Dermot Cassidy, 54 Bayview Avenue). The entire estate worth £420 was bequeathed to his son John.
2. *The Freeman's Journal*, 12 February 1873.
3. MacThomáis, *Me Jewel and Darlin' Dublin*, p. 94.
4. Ordnance Survey Map, 1847, Sheet XIV, Post Office Ward (TCML).
5. John W. DeCourcy, 'Bluffs, Bays and Pools in the Medieval Liffey at Dublin', *Irish Geography*, 33 (2) (2000): 117–33.
6. Damer House Papers, Indenture of lease dated 22 May 1755 (NLI Ms. 20840/2).
7. Seamus Scully, 'Around Dominick Street', *Dublin Historical Record*, 33 (3) (1980): 82–92.
8. Chief Superintendent Ryan to Police Commissioner, 8 April 1872 (NAI Fenian Papers, Carton 17/8130).
9. This is confirmed by reference to the Charles E. Goad insurance map for April 1926.
10. Peter J. Drumm and William F. O'Connor, 'The Production of Santonin from Irish Grown Artemesia', *Scientific Proceedings of the Royal Dublin Society*, 22 (13 June 1942): 279–82.
11. Memorial of a Deed of Conveyance, 31 July 1862 (ROD, Book 27/82).
12. Nicholas Mooney, *The Life of Nicholas Mooney, Alias Jackson, Born at Regar, Near Rathfarnham in the County of Dublin: Whereas Contained an Account of His Parentage and Education* (Dublin, 1752), p. 8.
13. *Dublin Mercury*, 9 June 1770.
14. Seamus Deane, Andrew Carpenter and Jonathan Williams, *The Field Day Anthology of Irish Writing, Irish Women's Writing and Traditions* (Cork, 2002), p. 66.
15. Andrew Kippis, *The New Annual Register, or, General Repository of History, Politics,*

and Literature for the Year 1784 (London, 1784), p. 57.

16. The Star, 19 July 1797.

17. The Sun, 5 May 1798.

18. The Sun, 11 June 1798.

19. Life, Trial and Conversations of Robert Emmet, Esq. (New York, 1845), p. 125.

20. Work Done for John Cash, Esq. at His 24 New-Built Houses in Cole's Market, Papers of Bryan Bolger, Measurer (NAI).

21. James Fraser, A Handbook for Travellers in Ireland (Dublin, 1844), p. 39.

22. The Freeman's Journal (Advertisement), 30 March 1838.

23. Just ten years earlier, in 1901, the percentage of the city's clothes dealers in Cole's Lane had stood at just under 13 per cent. The fact that this figure had increased to 25 per cent in 1911 demonstrates the increasing popularity of second-hand garments as mass production made castaway items more available to the poor.

24. Kevin C. Kearns, Dublin Tenement Life: An Oral History (Dublin, 1994), p. 34.

25. This can be seen on the Charles E. Goad Insurance Map, April 1926, Sheet No. 7 (TCML).

26. 'Royal Irish Academy List of Members', Proceedings of the Royal Irish Academy, 1836–1869, vol. 7 (1857–61), pp. 1–22.

27. Ordnance Survey Map, 1847, Sheet XIV, Post Office Ward (TCML).

28. Ordnance Survey Map, 1866, Sheet XIV (General Post Office) (TCML).

29. Henry Shaw's Dublin Pictorial Guide & Directory, 1850.

30. Newcastle Courant, 17 November 1871.

31. Meeting of the Corporation for paving the streets of Dublin (Dublin, 1782), p. 45.

32. John Cowell, Dublin's Famous People and Where They Lived (Dublin, 1996), p. 113.

33. Hull Packet and Original Commercial Weekly, 14 July 1818.

34. Dublin Directory, 1778.

35. Christine Casey, Dublin: The City within the Grand and Royal Canals and the Circular Road (London, 2005), p. 107.

36. Memorial of Indenture of Lease, 7 March 1803 (ROD Book 582, p. 486, no. 395373), Memorial of Indenture of Lease, 29 March 1805 (ROD Book 576, p. 65, no. 384877) and Memorial of an Indenture of Deed of Conveyance, 30 August 1844 (ROD no. 266).

37. Endymion, Seven Days in Dublin (Dublin, 1960).

38. The Irish Times, 4 November 1968.

39. The Natural Resources of Ireland: A Series of Discourses Delivered Before the Royal Dublin Society on April 12th, 13th, and 14th, 1944 in Commemoration of the Centenary of the Publication by the Society of Sir Robert Kane's 'The Industrial Resources of Ireland' (Dublin, 1944), p. 5.

40. Letter to Mr Swan of Damer House from Elizabeth Collins, 21 Denmark Street, 17 March 1832 (NLI Ms. 20840/2).

41. The Irish Times, 16 April 1931.

42. Timothy Dawson, 'Crane Lane to Ballybough', Dublin Historical Record, 27 (4) (1974): 131–45.

43. Sixty-Ninth Annual Report of the Commissioners of Charitable Donations and Bequests for Ireland, 1914, available online at http://pdf.library.soton.ac.uk/EPPI/15568.pdf (accessed 16 April 2012).

44. The Irish Times, 18 April 1911.

45. The Irish Times, 4 November 1968.

46. Robert Gahan, 'Old Alms-Houses of Dublin', Dublin Historical Record, 5 (1) (1942): 15–40.

47. Warburton et al., History of the City of Dublin.

48. The Irish Times, 3 October 1904.

49. The Irish Times, 26 January 1914.

50. 'Report of Registrar of Friendly Societies in Ireland', 1872, available online at http://pdf.library.soton.ac.uk/EPPI/8044.pdf (accessed 16 April 2012).

51. John W. Boyle, The Irish Labour Movement (Washington DC, 1988), p. 141.

52. The Irish Times, 8 November 1957.

53. The Irish Times, 18 October 1868.

54. Maurice Anthony Coneys Gorham, Forty Years of Irish Broadcasting (Dublin, 1967), pp. 21 & 25.

55. Ordnance Survey Map, 1866, Sheet XIV (General Post Office) (TCML).

56. The Freeman's Journal, 4 December 1879.

57. Griffith's Primary Valuation of Tenements, North City Ward, 1848–64 (NAI).

58. Charles E. Goad Insurance Map, Sheet No. 7 (TCML).

59. C. T. McCready, Dublin Street Names

(Dublin, 1892).

60. UCD, *Moore Street – A Report*, p. 5.

61. Kenneth Sheils Reddin, *Young Man with a Dream: A Novel* (New York, 1946), p. 196.

62. Seán O'Casey, *Pictures in the Hallway* (London, 1942), p. 127.

63. McCready, *Dublin Street Names*.

64. Ordnance Survey Map, 1847, Sheet XIV, Post Office Ward (TCML).

65. Seamus Scully, 'The Rotunda Gardens and Buildings', *Dublin Historical Record*, 34 (3) (1981): 110–20.

66. Philip H. Highfill, Kalman A. Burnim and Edward A. Langhans, *A Biographical Dictionary of Actors, Actresses, Musicians, Dancers, Managers and Other Stage Personnel in London, 1660–1800*, vol. XVI (Carbondale, Ill., 1993), p. 125; and Cowell, *Dublin's Famous People and Where They Lived*, p. 53.

67. Memorial of a Deed of Conveyance, 31 July 1862 (ROD, Book 27/82).

68. Memorial of an Indenture, 31 July 1862 (ROD, Book 27/83).

69. Ordnance Survey Map, 1866, Sheet XIV (General Post Office) (TCML).

70. *The Irish Times*, 8 January 1881.

71. Warburton *et al.*, *History of the City of Dublin*.

72. *The Irish Times*, 3 September 1904.

73. Peter Pearson, *The Heart of Dublin: Resurgence of an Historic City* (Dublin, 2000), p. 427. These buildings can be seen lining the northern side of the street on Charles E. Goad's insurance map of 1926.

74. Douglas Bennett, *The Encyclopaedia of Dublin* (Dublin, 2005), p. 243.

75. Dawson, 'Crane Lane to Ballybough'.

76. Damer House Papers, Reports on Conduct of Residents, 1829–32 (NLI, Ms. 20840/2).

77. Warburton *et al.*, *History of the City of Dublin*, p. 782.

78. Augustine Dillon Cosgrave, 'North Dublin City', *Dublin Historical Record*, 23 (1) (1969): 3–22.

79. Pearson, *The Heart of Dublin*, p. 407.

80. Primary Valuation of Tenements, St Mary's Parish, Dublin.

81. Ordnance Survey Map, 1847, Sheet XIV, Post Office Ward (TCML).

82. Walter Harris, *The History and Antiquities of the City of Dublin, from the Earliest Accounts; Compiled from Authentic Memoirs, Offices of Record, Manuscript Collections, and Other Unexceptionable Vouchers* (Dublin, 1766).

83. Jacqueline R. Hill, *From Patriots to Unionists: Dublin Civic Politics and Irish Protestant Patriotism, 1660–1840* (Oxford, 1997), p. 249.

84. *The Freeman's Journal*, 16 May 1833.

85. Andrew Hadfield and John McVeigh (eds), *Strangers to that Land: British Perceptions of Ireland from the Reformation* (Gerrard's Cross, 1994), p. 222.

86. Hill, *From Patriots to Unionists*, p. 336.

87. Griffith's Primary Valuation of Tenements, North City Ward, 1848–64 (NAI).

88. *The Freeman's Journal*, 10 December 1839.

89. Memorial of an Indenture, 24 November 1921 (ROD Book 74/280).

90. William Butler Yeats, *New Poems* (Dublin, 1938).

91. Memorial of an Indenture of Lease, 30 July 1714 (ROD Book 13, p. 323, no. 5840).

92. William McGavin, *The Protestant: A Series of Essays on the Principal Points of Controversy Between the Romish and Reformed Churches* (Glasgow, 1837).

93. *The Irish Times*, 29 June 1908.

94. *Irish Builder*, 5 July 1913.

95. *The Freeman's Journal*, 3 April 1830.

96. Prunty, *Dublin Slums, 1800–1925*, p. 324.

97. Charles E. Goad Insurance Map, April 1926, Sheet 7 (TCML).

Bibliography

Primary sources

Gilbert Library, Dublin

Meeting of the Corporation for paving the streets of Dublin (Dublin, 1781)
Meeting of the Corporation for paving the streets of Dublin (Dublin, 1782)
Calendar of Ancient Records of Dublin, vol. XIV, Lady Gilbert, ed. (Dublin, 1909)
Dublin Corporation Reports & c., Byelaws with respect to Slaughterhouses, 1879

Military Archives (Ireland)

Bureau of Military History witness statements

National Archives of Ireland

Card Catalogue of 1916 Internees
Chief Secretary Office Registered Papers (CSORP)
Crime Branch Special Papers
Fenian Papers
Griffith's Primary Valuation of Tenements, North City Ward
Minute Book of Directors of the Watch, 1750–70
1901 & 1911 Census of Ireland
Papers of Bryan Bolger, Measurer
Property Losses (Ireland) Committee, 1916
Report to Chief Secretary

National Library of Ireland

Damer House Papers, Ms. 20840/2
Sketch of Easter Week Operations in the GPO Area by Diarmuid Lynch, Ms. 5173
Henry Shaw's Dublin Pictorial Guide & Directory, 1850
Thom's Directory

Registry of Deeds, Dublin

Memorial of an indenture of lease, 30 July 1714 (Book 13, p. 323, no. 5840)
Memorial of an indenture of lease, 7 March 1803 (Book 582, p. 486, no. 395373)
Memorial of an indenture of lease, 29 March 1805 (Book 576, p. 65, no. 384877)
Memorial of an indenture of deed of conveyance, 30 August 1844 (no. 266)
Memorial of a deed of conveyance, 31 July 1862 (Book 27/82)
Memorial of an indenture, 24 November 1921 (Book 74/280)

Royal Dublin Society

The Natural Resources of Ireland: A series of discourses delivered before the Royal Dublin Society on April 12th, 13th, and 14th, 1944 in commemoration of the centenary of the publication by the Society of Sir Robert Kane's 'The Industrial Resources of Ireland'

Drumm, Peter J. and William F. O'Connor, 'The Production of Santonin from Irish Grown Artemesia', *Scientific Proceedings of the Royal Dublin Society*, 22 (13 June 1942): 279–82

Royal Irish Academy

Proceedings of the Royal Irish Academy, 1836–1869, vol. VII (1857–61)

Trinity College Map Library

Ordnance Survey Map, Sheet XIV, Post Office Ward, 1847
Ordnance Survey Map, Sheet XIV (General Post Office), 1866
Charles E. Goad Insurance Map, April 1926, Sheet No. 7
Charles E. Goad Insurance Map, 1957, Sheet No. 7

Secondary sources

Abrams, Charles, *Urban Renewal Project in Ireland* (Dublin and New York, 1961)

Behan, Dominic, *Teems of Times and Happy Returns* (Dublin, 1979)

Bennett, Douglas, *The Encyclopaedia of Dublin* (Dublin, 2005)

Boyle, John W., *The Irish Labour Movement* (Washington DC, 1988)

Casey, Christine, *Dublin: The City within the Grand and Royal Canals and the Circular Road* (London, 2005)

Collins, Lorcan and Conor Kostick, *The Easter Rising* (Dublin, 2001)

Coneys Gorham, Maurice Anthony, *Forty Years of Irish Broadcasting* (Dublin, 1967)

Connor, James A., 'Radio Free Joyce: "Wake" Language and the Experience of Radio', *James Joyce Quarterly*, 31 (1) (1993): 825–43

Cowell, John, *Dublin's Famous People and Where They Lived*, 2nd edn (Dublin, 1996)

Cronin, Seán, *Young Connolly* (Dublin, 1978)

Cruise O'Brien, Conor, 'Passion and Cunning: An Essay on the Politics of W. B. Yeats', in Jonathan Allison (ed.), *Yeats's Political Identities: Selected Essays* (Michigan, 1996), pp. 29–44

Cullen, Bill, *It's a Long Way from Penny Apples* (Cork, 2002)

Dawson, Timothy, 'Crane Lane to Ballybough', *Dublin Historical Record*, 27 (4) (1974): 131–45

Deane, Seamus, Andrew Carpenter, and Jonathan Williams (eds), *The Field Day Anthology of Irish Writing*, vols IV and V: *Irish Women's Writing and Traditions* (Cork, 2002)

DeCourcy, John W., 'Bluffs, Bays and Pools in the Medieval Liffey at Dublin', *Irish Geography*, 33 (2) (2000): 117–33

Dillon Cosgrave, Augustine, 'North Dublin City', *Dublin Historical Record*, 23 (1) (1969): 3–22

Endymion, *Seven Days in Dublin* (Dublin, 1960)

Foy, Michael T. and Brian Barton, *The Easter Rising* (Stroud, 1999)

Fraser, James, *A Handbook for Travellers in Ireland* (Dublin, 1844)

Gahan, Robert, 'Old Alms-Houses of Dublin', *Dublin Historical Record*, 5 (1) (1942): 15–40

Geraghty, Tom and Trevor Whitehead, *The Dublin Fire Brigade: A History of the Brigade, the Fires and the Emergencies* (Dublin, 2004)

Gray, Henry Colin Matthew and Brian Howard Harrison, *Oxford Dictionary of National Biography* (Oxford, 2004)

Hadfield, Andrew and John McVeigh (eds), *Strangers to that Land: British Perceptions of Ireland from the Reformation* (Gerrard's Cross, 1994)

Harris, Walter, *The History and Antiquities of the City of Dublin, from the Earliest Accounts; Compiled from Authentic Memoirs, Offices of Record, Manuscript Collections, and Other Unexceptionable Vouchers* (Dublin, 1766)

Henderson, Frank and Michael Hopkinson (ed.), *Frank Henderson's Easter Rising: Recollections of a Dublin Volunteer* (Cork, 1998)

Highfill, Philip H., Kalman A. Burnim and Edward A. Langhans, *A Biographical Dictionary of Actors, Actresses, Musicians, Dancers, Managers and Other Stage Personnel in London, 1660–1800*, vol. XVI (Carbondale, Ill., 1993)

Hill, Jacqueline R., *From Patriots to Unionists: Dublin Civic Politics and Irish Protestant Patriotism, 1660–1840* (Oxford, 1997)

Kearns, Kevin C., *Dublin Tenement Life: An Oral History* (Dublin, 1994)

Kippis, Andrew, *The New Annual Register, or, General Repository of History, Politics, and Literature for the Year 1784* (London, 1784)

Kissane, Noel (compiler), *Historic Dublin Maps* (Dublin, 1988)

Liddy, Pat, *Dublin Be Proud* (Dublin, 1987)

Life, Trial and Conversations of Robert Emmet, Esq. (New York, 1845)

MacEntee, Seán, *Episode at Easter* (Dublin and Melbourne, 1966)

MacThomáis, Éamonn, *Me Jewel and Darlin' Dublin* (Dublin, 1974)

McCready, C. T., *Dublin Street Names* (Dublin, 1892)

McDonald, Frank, *The Destruction of Dublin* (Dublin, 1985)

McGarry, Fearghal, *The Rising: Ireland, Easter 1916* (Oxford, 2010)

McGavin, William, *The Protestant: A Series of Essays on the Principal Points of Controversy Between the Romish and Reformed Churches* (Glasgow, 1837)

McGuire, Charlie, 'Seán McLoughlin: The Boy Commandant of 1916', *History Ireland*, 14 (2) (2006) (1916: 90th Anniversary Issue): 26–30

Mooney, Nicholas, *The Life of Nicholas Mooney, Alias Jackson, Born at Regar, Near Rathfarnham in the County of Dublin: Whereas Contained an Account of His Parentage and Education* (Dublin, 1752)

O'Beirne, Michael, 'There's no place like Moore Street', *The Irish Digest*, 73 (2) (1961): 34–5

—— *And the Moon at Night: A Dubliner's Story* (Belfast, 1981)

O'Casey, Seán, *The Plough and the Stars: A Tragedy in Four Acts* (London, 1930)

—— *Pictures in the Hallway* (London, 1942)

Pearson, Peter, *The Heart of Dublin: Resurgence of an Historic City* (Dublin, 2000)

Prunty, Jacinta, *Dublin Slums, 1800–1925: A Study in Urban Geography* (Dublin, 1998)

Sawden Pritchett, Victor, *Dublin: A Portrait* (London, 1967)

Scully, Seamus, 'Ghosts of Moore Street', *Dublin Historical Record*, 25 (2) (1972): 54–63

—— 'Around Dominick Street', *Dublin Historical Record*, 33 (3) (1980): 82–92

—— 'The Rotunda Gardens and Buildings', *Dublin Historical Record*, 34 (3) (1981): 110–20

—— 'Moore Street – 1916', *Dublin Historical Record*, 39 (2) (1986): 53–63

—— *The Dublin Rover* (Dublin, 1991)

Sheils Reddin, Kenneth, *Young Man with a Dream: A Novel* (New York, 1946)

Sinn Féin Rebellion Handbook, compiled by weekly *Irish Times* (Dublin, 1917)

Tynan, Catherine, *The Years of the Shadow* (London, 1919)

UCD School of Architecture, *Moore Street – A Report* (Dublin, 1974)

Warburton, John, James Whitelaw and Robert Walsh, *History of the City of Dublin: From the Earliest Accounts to the Present Time: Containing Its Annals to Which Are Added, Biographical Notices of Eminent Men*, vol. II (Dublin, 1818)

Whitelaw, James, *An Essay on the Population of Dublin, Being the Result of an Actual Survey Taken in 1798* (Dublin, 1805)

—— *An Account of the Enumeration of the Inhabitants of the City of Dublin* (Dublin, 1805)

Yeats, William Butler, *New Poems* (Dublin, 1938)

Videos

Bananas on a Breadboard: Stories from the Market Area, Dublin (Dublin City Council, 2009)

John Walters, *Business as Usual* (IADT, National Film School, Dublin, 2010)

Websites

House of Commons Parliamentary Debate, 1 August 1916, vol. 85, ccl 23–256. Available online at http://hansard.millbanksystems.com (accessed May 2011)

Moore Street Masala, 4 August 2009. Available online at http://www.screenscene.ie/index.php?/grade_and_telecine/moore_street_masala/ (accessed 16 April 2012)

Report of Registrar of Friendly Societies in Ireland, 1872. Available online at http://www-lib.soton.ac.uk (accessed 16 April 2012)

Seamus Marken Remembers the Sounds of Moore Street (Trinity College Dublin, *Lifescapes: Mapping Dublin Lives*). Accessed in May 2011 online at http://bridge-it.tchpc.tcd.ie

Sixty-Ninth Annual Report of the Commissioners of Charitable Donations and Bequests for Ireland for the year ended 31 December, 1913. Available online at http://pdf.library.soton.ac.uk/EPPI/15568.pdf (accessed 16 April 2012)

Newspapers, periodicals and journals

Caledonian Mercury

Catholic Bulletin

Dublin Builder, The

Dublin Directory

Dublin Mercury

Dublin Monthly Magazine

Dublin Warder

Freeman's Journal, The

Hull Packet and Commercial Weekly

Irish Builder

Irish Independent

Irish Press
Irish Times, The
Liverpool Mercury
Newcastle Courant
Protestant Penny Magazine
Star, The
Sun, The
Sunday Independent
Weekly News, The

Interviews

Interview with Maureen Kennerk, 1 October 2010
Interview with Ken Robinson, 13 May 2011
Interview with Bill Cullen, 18 May 2011
Interview with Jack Kennerk, 16 June 2011
Interview with May Gorman, 27 June 2011
Interview with Bernie Shea, 17 November 2011
Interview with Justin Leonard, 18 November 2011
Interview with Catherine Hansard, 23 November 2011
Interview with Seanie Lambe, 23 November 2011
Interview with Brendan Egan, 25 November 2011
Interview with Seamus Marken, 26 November 2011
Interview with P. J. Gallagher, 10 December 2011
Interview with Salim Ullah Khan, 10 December 2011
Interview with Seamus O'Rourke, 12 December 2011
Interview with Martin (Willie) Higgins, 21 December 2011
Interview with Catherine (Kitty) Campion, 23 December 2011
Interview with Alice Dardis, 2 January 2012
Interview with Eamon Martin, 6 January 2012
Interview with Stevo Lynch, 10 January 2012
Interview with Paddy Ormsby, 16 January 2012
Interview with Garrett Keogh, 21 January 2012
Interview with Christy O'Leary and John Igoe, 23 January 2012
Interview with Patrick Cooney, 29 January 2012
Interview with Keith Duffy, 8 March 2012
Interview with Davy Byrne, 12 May 2012